MAGICAL LOVE MESSAGES
BETWEEN KINDRED SPIRITS

MAGICAL LOVE MESSAGES BETWEEN KINDRED SPIRITS

HEATHER D. WRIGHT

COLORFUL SPIRIT PUBLISHING
Boone

Contents

Title   xi

Magical Love Messages Between Kindred Spirits   xi

Copyright Information   xii

Dedication & Introduction   xiii

Chapter 1 - A Destined Love Story Between a Magical Muse and a Struggling Artist   1

Chapter 2 - A Karmic Love Story   6

Chapter 3 - A Love Letter from Another Time and Place   10

Chapter 4 - A Magical Connection on a Brand New Path   14

Chapter 5 - A Mystical Love From a Spiritual Place   19

Chapter 6 - A Special Kind of Love Between Kindred Spirits   23

Chapter 7 - A Timeless Love Letter 27

Chapter 8 - A Trusted Friend to the End 31

Chapter 9 - An Agape Kind of Love 36

Chapter 10 - An Enchanting Tale
Between Two Kindred Souls 41

Chapter 11 - An Unbreakable
Connection Between Twin Souls 45

Chapter 12 - Finding Refuge in a
Soulmate's Heart 49

Chapter 13 - I Love the Way 54

Chapter 14 - Magical Ties Through
Mystical Times 59

Chapter 15 - My Soul Cat and Me 63

Chapter 16 - The Butterfly that Became
My Friend 68

Chapter 17 - The Coloring Box of Love 72

Chapter 18 - The Comforting Scratch on
the Door 75

Chapter 19 - The Day Fear Took a
Chance on Love 78

Chapter 20 - The Day Sad Fell in Love
With Happy 82

Chapter 21 - The Deep Breath Between   87
Soulmates

Chapter 22 - The Enduring Spirit of Love   91
Through Nine Lives

Chapter 23 - The Healing Nature of a   94
Soulmate's Touch

Chapter 24 - The Home that Kept Us   98
Together

Chapter 25 - The Homeless Friend I Call   102
Sunset

Chapter 26 - The Leaves of Love   106

Chapter 27 - The Life Raft and the   110
Yellow Bird that Saved My Soul

Chapter 28 - The Little Yellow Bird With   114
the Key to My Heart

Chapter 29 - The Love Story Between a   118
Seagull and a Broken Soul

Chapter 30 - The Lover of My Soul   122

Chapter 31 - The Loving Link Between   126
Kindred Souls

Chapter 32 - The Magical Love Destiny   130
Between Twin Souls

Chapter 33 - The Music Box Connection   134

Chapter 34 - The Mysterious Cat and   138
Two Connected Spirits

Chapter 35 - The Night a Soulmate   142
Rescued My Heart

Chapter 36 - The Painting on the Wall   146

Chapter 37 - The Past Life Love   150
Connection

Chapter 38 - The Poetic Song Between   154
Kindred Spirits

Chapter 39 - The Rainbow Bridge to a   157
Truly Missed Friend

Chapter 40 - The Red-winged Black Bird   161
With a Special Kind of Love

Chapter 41 - The Soulmate Adventure   165

Chapter 42 - The Soulmate Protector   169

Chapter 43 - The Soulmate Rescue   173

Chapter 44 - The Special Friend that   177
Took a Lost Child By the Hand

Chapter 45 - The Special Friendship   182
Between a Seagull and a Starfish

Chapter 46 - The Time Machine Back to   186
a Fairy Tale Kind of Life

Chapter 47 - The True Soul Friend   190

Chapter 48 - To Mom and Dad With Love   193

Chapter 49 - Two Trees Linked by a Loving Connection   197

Chapter 50 - With Love From Mr. Goodbar   201

Afterword   205
About the Author   207

Title

Magical Love Messages Between Kindred Spirits

by Heather D. Wright

Courtesy of Colorful Spirit Publishing

Copyright Information

Dedication & Introduction

This book is dedicated to God and to all those kindred spirits out there because without you this book would not have been possible. The creative inspiration I received when writing this book was truly divine intervention.

Love is the one thing so many of us desire to have in our lives, and yet, it is the one thing we so often fail to achieve. Sometimes we think we have to do or say something to earn someone's love when what we fail to realize is that love, first and foremost, comes from God. Every kind of love we feel and share with others is a result of our spiritual connection to a power much greater and stronger than all of us.

When reflecting on the nature of this book, I wanted to share many poetic works I have drafted in the realm of love and friendship. I feel they are two sides of the same coin and the very things we need to sustain us and give us life. When it comes to matters of the heart, I have truly had some interesting experiences, so many of which I did not understand, yet the lessons I learned were profound.

The one thing I have learned is that love exists in many different ways and in many diverse forms in the areas of spiritual connections. Through the power of kindred spirits, I have come to feel the kind of love God wants each of us to enjoy and experience. I have heard that it is better to have loved and lost then to have never loved at all, and through the content of this book, you will feel the great power of love in many unique ways.

If you feel a lack of love in your life or feel you have not experienced the power of spiritual love in its greatest form, I sincerely hope you will enjoy this book, Magical Love Messages Between Kindred Spirits, as each chapter contains a special message of love that will transform your life and your connections with those to whom you feel special ties.

Chapter 1 – A Destined Love Story Between a Magical Muse and a Struggling Artist

———————

Magical Message #1 – Destiny plays a creative role in special souls we meet.

Ever wonder why you meet the people you do? Sometimes people come and go into our lives. We often do not understand why we are meant to meet the people that we do. However, every so often someone comes along whom we are destined to meet and who will change our lives forever. I have learned not to question anyone who comes into my life. Even at times when I do not understand the purpose that person may fulfill, I know there is a reason he or she has crossed my path.

The following poem, "A Destined Love Story Between

a Magical Muse and A Struggling Artist", is about two people, a magical muse who is creative and dances to the joyous music of life, and a struggling artist, whose desire to sell his inspirational works keeps him wanting to be a success. However, in this poem, the artist feels he is often uninspired and needing something to help keep his creative juices flowing. At the moment when he is most ready to give up, destiny leads him to a beautiful muse whose enthusiasm and positive outlook on life gives him hope to stand strong and not give up on his dreams.

For anyone needing inspiration to pursue your dreams, keep the faith that one day God will lead you to your own special muse meant to encourage the path upon which God is leading you.

A Destined Love Story Between a Magical Muse and A Struggling Artist

I was deep in a dream wondering
What my life was meant to be
Somewhere in the depths of my soul
I could feel my true love sharing in my destiny

In a moment I was brought to a place
Where I struggled to create paintings meant to inspire
Yet I could not make ends meet with my artistic
Efforts leaving me frustrated and always so tired

MAGICAL LOVE MESSAGES BETWEEN KINDRED SPIRITS

I was ready to give up because I felt it was hopeless
To keep going with such little motivation
Then one day as I was walking a lovely soul greeted
Me upon my path with an enticing invitation

I followed him to a gallery where brilliant minds
Had created the most elegant works of art
The spirit who had crossed my path whispered
You have lots to give so always follow your heart

As I went to explore more of the creative
Flow of energy surrounding my soul
I noticed my new spiritual muse disappeared and
I knew I needed him too much to let him go

I began my search as I felt determined to
Find the key to a new lease on life
Then I walked into a building where the Spirit who
Greeted me was dancing nicely so I could not pass him by

He invited me to dance along side of him to
Feel the energy that lit up the room where he danced
Somehow he could look into my eyes with great hope
Giving my dying spirit a brand new chance

My new friend told me he was a magical muse
Sent to inspire me to never let my talents fall apart
With great enthusiasm I felt our destined meeting
Was orchestrated with a language from the heart

___

The magical muse took my hand and showed me
Where our true souls could be free
I wanted to make this happen with you by my side
Because without you I will fall victim again to misery

Excited and ready to explore a new place where
Dreams and visions could come true
My magical muse said I support you always
But it is time I go away far from you

Confused and not sure of why the muse I had
Come to love so much would leave me alone
I knew that I had to go find him again
So my heart would find its true home

After a long journey of creating an artistic haven
Where creative ideas would never die
God helped me bridge the gap into his world
With nothing holding me back and no reasons to ask why

His family and friends did not want him to
Leave the place where they felt he should stay
But my love for him and the dance of mutual trust
Between us could not let me walk away

When I took my charming muse by the hand
To come back into the special world we had created
I could feel my hopes were finally met as the love
We shared kept me feeling strong and elated

MAGICAL LOVE MESSAGES BETWEEN KINDRED SPIRITS

As days and nights have passed by I can still remember
Dancing with my muse from dusk to dawn
We lived in a world where artistic talent
Kept us hopeful and singing our own special love songs

The memories from this past life still exist in my soul
When I see artwork or people dancing together
I can still feel the love and creative energy
We shared keeping us bonded forever

Chapter 2 - A Karmic Love Story

_____

Magical Message #2 – Remember that love exists
in the most unconventional places.

Love is truly the most desired emotion, and yet, it is often the one that is the hardest for anyone of us to really experience. Everyday people search for the kind of love that will never fail, a love that is strong enough to surpass obstacles and hard times no matter what. In life, some people long to be loved so much, but often have been so hurt by those with whom they felt really loved them with great joy and no regrets.

The following poem, "A Karmic Love Story", is a story about one soul's search for a love that he discovers in the most unique of places. Often we try to put labels on love, and we try to make it seem that if a certain person does not meet up to our family expectations, that this person

is not acceptable. However, in the poem below, there is a
love that exists among souls who maybe at one point or
another were disconnected from each other in the past,
and yet through time, rediscover the love that once lost
never really died.

A Karmic Love Story

Once upon a time in a place
Far and away that nobody could find
There lived a lonely soul who felt he needed
To find love before he ran out of time

He searched the world over and never
Quite knew where his answer could be
All he knew was he felt driven by a thirst
To find the other half of his karmic destiny

It seemed so many years had passed
And he never could find the secret to his heart's story
Every moment that passed was just another second
Wasted and time lost to misguided worry

In the midst of his search, he knew that he needed
To find a way to make his life complete
Somehow his journey into his thoughts was
A time for him to overcome all defeat

Through daydreams the lonely soul imagined
What it would be like to meet his karmic friend

In his visions he could feel the warm embrace of
A kindred spirit loving him over and over again

As he went through the daily motions
Of his often stifling routine
He could hear his soul crying out
For someone to love him unconditionally

In the break of dawn when the sun would
Embrace the horizon with its ray of light
The desperate soul could see a glimpse of a new day
To remind him that everything would be all right

In the evening when he was driving home from
A long day of relentless stress he wanted to forget
He was greeted by an artistic sunset that seemed
To have the calming force to soothe all his regrets

As he lay his head down every night
In the hopes to get some sleep
He was often greeted by an angelic presence
Full of great joy and love with eyes full of peace

In his dream he reached for the hand of the woman
Who seemed to understand him so well
She whispered in his ears if you come walk with me
I will always have special stories to tell

It was hard to wake up and face
All the obstacles that came his way

Yet somehow the lonely soul knew
He had to keep searching for his karmic partner everyday

On a journey through a field
Out in a meadow nearby
He came across a letter lying in the grass
With some writing that immediately caught his eye

As he picked up the letter and read the words
That seemed to be a mystery
The words he read said, "I will love you forever
From now through eternity"

The lonely soul walked around for hours to see
If he could find the author to such powerful words
Yet he knew his heart was no longer as empty
Because the words above put an end to his broken world

As he closed his eyes he could feel that
Something in his life was no longer the same
After all his long days and nights of searching
For his one true love, he felt no more shame

In the midst of a gentle breeze, the brand new soul
Swayed in peace with his hand over his heart
From this moment on he knew he had found
A spiritual love that would never fall apart

Chapter 3 - A Love Letter from Another Time and Place

———————

Magical Message #3 – Trust your instincts when you feel drawn to someone or something that feeds your soul.

Intuition is a powerful force in our lives. Sometimes we need to feel a connection with something deeper, something that reminds us that we are never really alone. I truly believe we have shared past lives with many different people. Whether we realize it or not, there may come a time when a simple object, whether a piece of artwork, a song, or even a simple letter takes us back to another time and place where someone that really loved us knew us before reconnecting in this lifetime. We may not remember all the details of the life we lived with that special soul that touched our lives. However, some how in some way, we feel that connection of love and friendship reminding us that we are never really alone on the road of life.

In the following poem, "A Love Letter From Another Time and Place", you will find a story of how one lonely soul discovered a message in a bottle connecting him to a special friend he had loved and lost in another lifetime. Even though his current memories of that lifetime do not exist, he can still feel the depth of caring and love that was felt between himself and his special friend from another time and place where life was simpler and more meaningful.

When you feel drawn to something or someone, trust your instincts because it could be the one moment your life is changed forever. It could be the time you realize there is a special feeling of love and trust that exists around you spiritually to help you feel loved and protected through all the good and bad times of this life.

A Love Letter from Another Time and Place

I was walking along a path one cool
Crisp evening in the fall
When I saw a message in a bottle with a curious
Letter within that I could not resist to read at all

As I opened this mystic bottle
To see what was inside

I could feel an amazing love come over me
Filling me with a warm feeling I hoped would never die

When I unfolded this intriguing letter
I was not sure what I was meant to know
But an inner voice inside whispered
I'm the love of your life that will never let you go

The words of this letter echoed in my spirit as follows...

"Dear Love, I have been wondering
Where could you have been?
I have looked the world over to feel the grace
of your touch like a long, awaited friend.

In every place I have lived
I could not rest without you there
Through all the battles I have been fighting
I knew I needed someone right beside me to always care.

You may not remember all the times
That we shared together
Yet I could feel inside we were meant
To love deeply through all the stormy weather.

There were moments that chains
Around my soul tried to break me down
But I could hold my hand over my heart
And feel your loving presence all around.

MAGICAL LOVE MESSAGES BETWEEN KINDRED SPIRITS

In the days when it seemed
I wanted to completely give up
You were the inner voice guiding me
To stay strong and have faith in better luck.

No matter what life I have lived
And no matter where the road of life has taken
I can reach inside my soul
And know you're with me without ever feeling mistaken."

As I came to the end of this touching letter
I could feel the energy of love leading me back home
The lover of my soul from another lifetime
Encouraged me to keep this letter without losing hope

Chapter 4 - A Magical Connection on a Brand New Path

Magical Message #4 – Don't be afraid to embrace new beginnings in your life.

We have all been there. We have all faced times when it seemed it would be much easier to stay right where we are than to find a new path. I have often been scared out of my mind to make changes because I always thought it would be easier to stay right where I am without ever trying to improve myself. Sometimes we all get stuck in a rut, but then we realize we have to keep the faith and try much harder to find a way to be happier. Life is truly short, and the longer we stay at the same place in our lives where we feel unfulfilled, the more apt we are to keep feeling sad and hopeless. I have learned though when I took a leap of faith

on a new journey in my life that often God sent something
or someone to help me along the way.

In the following poem, "A Magical Connection on a Brand
New Path", you will find the story of one soul who is rather
tired of his life. This soul feels nobody truly cares for
him let alone understand the emptiness in his spirit. After
being frustrated for so long, this soul decides to take a new
path for his life in the hopes of getting the help he needs.
Before long he meets a special red bird whose simple
presence and wings of hope encourage him to soul search
for meaning in his life. This red bird encourages the
broken soul to not lose heart and to know that even during
moments he feels nobody truly cares, there does exist a
friend who will stay right by his side.

Sometimes in this life all it takes is someone or something
to just show us we are loved knowing we have a true friend
to help us keep going when we just want to give up.

A Magical Connection on a Brand New Path

I was walking along a path in the woods
Trying to hide from it all
I had reached my limits with fake promises and people
Pretending to care with all their fake talk

Somewhere in the midst of this path I asked God
Why I was always the one being attacked

He just whispered down to me quit thinking like
You are defeated and stop looking back

With tears of frustration I decided maybe nobody
Would ever understand who I truly am
It seemed I had spent years searching for one
Special soul who somehow could understand

As I walked a little further down this path
That was my escape from reality
There was a desire within to find something
To help me cope with life's misery

I was lost in despair thinking maybe it was time for me
To just quit trying to figure out why
Then I saw a red bird watching over me
As if to give solace to my weary cries

For some reason I felt this red bird may have been
A sign sent from God to help me on my path
So I asked this bird why I felt broken
And how I needed to get back on track

This special red bird could not speak, but his bright eyes
Connected with me in such a powerful way
As I stared into his eyes I saw a reflection of a soul
That seemed to love me deeply with great faith

Somehow I could not understand why I felt so drawn
To this special red bird I just met

However, the longer I watched him he flapped his wings
As if to say the best is to come yet

I decided that I needed to keep walking on this new path
Because somehow I did not feel as alone
This special red bird flew from one tree after the other
As if to say I am your true home

In a matter of minutes my tears quickly
Faded into a nice, warm smile
The special red bird somehow knew I needed
A loving friend to help me feel more worthwhile

I could not figure out why this special red bird
Stayed so closely by me as I kept walking this trail
It was as if he carried the spirit of a past life love
Encouraging me when I thought I would fail

After a long walk on this path, I felt maybe
I needed to take a short break
I sat down right in the middle of the trail trying
To make sense of all my past mistakes

When I looked around the special red bird
Had come to sit right by my weary side
It just sat peacefully beside me as if to say
I truly love you and want to help you release your pride

As I placed my hand over my heart I could feel a pain
Within that I so needed to release

When I looked into the bird's eyes I saw an image
Of my true love setting my soul at ease

I wanted so badly to reach out and give this
Bright red bird a special embrace
Yet all I could do was look deeply into his eyes
And know we were connected in magical ways

Even though I was in the process of searching my soul
To find some answers to my questions
I knew I could get back on my feet again
And travel this new path with much more direction

As I took the next few steps down this path
That somehow had changed my life
I looked up and saw the special red bird flying
Right above to keep me safe from unwanted strife

Even though I was not sure where God
Had intended for me to go
I knew I found a magical connection linking me
To a new friend whose love strengthened my soul

Chapter 5 - A Mystical Love From a Spiritual Place

Magical Message #5 – Sometimes love comes to protect us in mysterious ways.

I have always believed God is in control of this world. His creation of nature is simply the most beautiful work of art that ever existed. It is amazing how a simple sunrise or sunset or even how certain birds or butterflies have a special way of conveying God's love for us. In fact, I also feel He sends us the loving energies and peace from those who have passed before us to comfort our wounded souls through the simple acts or creations of nature.

The following poem, "A Mystical Love from a Spiritual Place", focuses on one person's journey to feel connected to something bigger than himself. This poem reflects one person's desire to feel truly loved in a world where he has come to feel so all alone. It is essentially a cry for help, and in the cry for help, God responds to this soul desperate for love by reaching out through mysterious ways to show him how much he is admired.

No matter how alone or lost you may be feeling, just keep the faith that some way some how God will send you a sign in the most unique ways that you are truly loved and protected.

A Mystical Love from a Spiritual Place

There are times I feel God taking me
On a brand new path
I feel Him leading me away from all the times
I felt broken from my difficult past

There are times I wonder when
The struggle will come to an end
I just put my head in my hands
And hope for the courage to try again

There are times I walk on so many
Paths trying to find my way
I just pray that God will give me peace
And not let me stray

There are times I pull the covers
Over my head at night

MAGICAL LOVE MESSAGES BETWEEN KINDRED SPIRITS

I wonder when all the bad times will be
Overcome by a much greater spiritual light

There are times I can feel someone
Touching the very depth of my soul
I am not sure from where it comes
But I know its a special love that will never let me go

There are times I sit in silence hoping all the setbacks
I face will one day make sense
I often do not know where I am heading
But God keeps me traveling in a direction meant for bliss

There are times I can look into the sky
And see birds flying with grace
That is when I can feel the freedom of a love
That surrounds me with wisdom and faith

There are times butterflies circle around me
With a delicate dance I have learned to trust
Even when times are hard they have a special way
Of healing my wounds with their colors of good luck

There are times I wander around
Feeling as lost as I can be
Then I look into a stream of water and see ducks
Floating side by side as if to say they love me

There are times I can feel pulled in so many directions
That I feel I am losing my mind

But somehow I can feel a warmth around my spirit
As a welcome voice that love is kind

There are times I lay my head down at night
Thinking of things I could have or should have done
Then I place my hand over my heart and feel a peace
Within that whispers the best is yet to come

There are times I know that letting go
And letting God win is my best course of action
With every heartbeat I keep the faith this mystical love
From a spiritual place is my best attraction

Chapter 6 – A Special Kind of Love Between Kindred Spirits

Magical Message #6 – Remember true spiritual love never fails and has the power to heal a wounded soul.

We all have been in need of someone to really care. Often in this life it can be a true struggle to find at least one person who knows us best and who has the right words at the right time to help us along life's way. There are many moments in life that we all just need at least one like minded soul who completes us and who knows how to love us on both our good and bad days.

I believe we all have special connections or what I call kindred spirits in our lives that could be a family member, a dear friend, or a romantic partner. A kindred spirit is one who loves us in the most unconditional and spiritual ways possible. It is truly a love from God that gives us the courage and strength to overcome our problems and to embrace better days that lie ahead.

The following poem, "A Special Love Between Kindred Spirits", is a reflection of the true nature of spiritual love that is forever and unfailing between two souls who share a beautiful connection.

A Special Kind of Love Between Kindred Spirits

I love you for just being there
When the right words are hard for me to say
I love you for just knowing how to smile at me
When my own sadness refuses to go away

I love you for just being able to connect
With my inner fears when I feel I cannot survive
I love you for helping me stand strong
When I feel too sick to even try

I love you for breathing new life into my restless soul
When I so often want to quit
I love you for knowing how to make me laugh
When my frustrating energies outweigh my own wit

I love you for feeling something is not right
Even though I often try to be on top of the world
I love you for helping me see that sometimes
It is ok to just be honest even when I feel so hurt

MAGICAL LOVE MESSAGES BETWEEN KINDRED SPIRITS

I love the magical ways you can light up a room
When everything else seems so chaotic
I love the moments the energy of great joy
Connects our spirits with a charm that is so hypnotic

I love the times I can count on you
To always be loyal and true
I love that no matter where my craziness takes me
You are always generous and forever cool

I love that when I want to run away
And never tell anyone where I am
I love that your energy caresses my desperate soul
With the kind of support only we can understand

I love you for always helping me heal
When my heart and soul seems shattered and worn
I love that when I am making hard decisions
I can look at you and not feel so troubled and torn

I love the special ways I can feel your presence
When I feel I am so alone even in a crowd
I love the way you can help me be strong
And courageous when I need to feel proud

I love the creative ways you can connect to my soul
Just to let me know you truly care
I love that you can send me spiritual signs
You will help me and always be there

I love the special kind of connection that keeps our souls
Close together through good and bad times
I just want to say that I love you so much for being
The kindred spirit whose heart remains forever kind

Chapter 7 - A Timeless Love Letter

Magical Message #7 – Some words are strong enough to heal a broken and longing heart.

There are times in this life when we all have felt truly alone and lost. There are times when it seems that nobody does understand who we really are. Our hearts feel alone, and then just when we think we can trust someone, that person lets us down.

I don't know much, but what I do know is that it is good to be aware of everything within your surroundings. If you find something that speaks to your soul, do not take it for granted. Anything you feel a pull to is meant to help change your life in great ways.

The following poem, "A Timeless Love Letter", focuses on a letter that helps heal the soul of one who is searching for a place to call home, a place where his heart feels whole again. Through the words of a mysterious love letter he finds in a bottle lying on the shore of beach, he realizes that he no longer has to feel so alone. His heart has found the key to the other half of his heart through a beautiful spiritual connection that was meant to last through eternity. Sometimes something as simple as a letter can impact us in the deepest ways possible.

A Timeless Love Letter

I was walking along the shore of a beach
Where I had traveled so many miles
I came across a message in a bottle that was
Buried in the sand, yet its presence made me all smiles

When I went to open the bottle to read
The great message I felt it contained
I could feel drawn to a special energy inside
That had been waiting to be claimed

As I unwrapped the paper inside this glass
That seemed worn with time
The first words on the letter seemed to
Reach the depth of my spirit with a harmonious rhyme

The greeting began
"To The Long Lost Love of My Life..."

MAGICAL LOVE MESSAGES BETWEEN KINDRED SPIRITS

Amazed at the words I read it was as if this may
Have been the answer to all of my present strife

I read a little further the words
"I have spent my whole life searching for you."
Then I kept reading more as the words came
"You were always the one that was true."

There was something unique about the next line that said
"You were the other half of me."
I then became spellbound by the next few words
"Without you my heart was left in misery."

Tears began to flood my eyes as I read the words
"Nothing matters but finding my lost soul."
Intrigued by this mystery, I kept reading
"I've loved you forever and never have let you go."

I wondered who could have written the words
"Please don't forget the magic we shared."
The more I kept reading, I heard the words on paper echo
"You were always the one who cared."

My heart beat more loudly as I read
"Please don't ever stop feeling my hand over your heart."
As I placed my hand on my heart these words hit my soul
"I have loved you from the start."

I could feel a magical power take over me as the words
"We have been connected forever."

Then joy came pouring over me through the words
"Our love will not be severed."

As I reached the last couple lines of this letter
"I need to feel your soul always connecting to mine."
My spirit started soaring with the remaining words
"I will love your forever until the end of time."

When I closed the letter and slipped it back
Into the bottle that changed my day
I looked up to God and cried please help me keep
The love of my life close to me in every way

Chapter 8 – A Trusted Friend to the End

Magical Message #8 – The value of true friendship is a bond that cannot be broken.

Friendship has always been a treasure to me. Throughout my entire life, God has blessed my path with the best of friends. I cannot imagine how empty my life would be without the gift of friends I could always trust. There are times when we all need to have friends, and yet, there are times we need to know we have at least one close friend we can trust with our deepest emotions and thoughts. I believe the best kind of friend is one that will love you no matter what, the kind of friend that encourages you to keep the faith when it seems the whole world is against you.

I find it sad that many people struggle to find a good friend because of the inability to trust due to being betrayed by someone you thought really cared. Learning who a true friend really is and learning what a true friend is not are the keys to finding someone who not only knows you best but who will never leave your side.

The following poem, "A Trusted Friend to the End", paints a true picture of the kind of friend we all long to have, the kind of friend we can trust and with whom we feel a special connection that never dies.

A Trusted Friend to the End

I was reaching high and low for
Something solid that I could trust
It seemed everything around me made me
Feel weak and left me feeling out of luck

I could walk down every street looking for
The right answers to all my questions
Yet I always met many thoughtless souls
Who led me astray with false promises and rejections

I often could feel the disappointment of
Many years of people letting me down
They promised to be there for me
Yet when I needed a friend they were nowhere to be found

In moments when it seemed that
My sad times would never end

MAGICAL LOVE MESSAGES BETWEEN KINDRED SPIRITS

I looked up and asked God when
He would send me a trustworthy, spiritual friend

In times of great storms all I wanted to do
Was find a refuge from the pain
I found myself feeling once again the
Victim of misfortune's misguided claim to fame

There were dark spirits lurking in the
Shadows of places where I wanted to feel safe
Yet in the midst of my despair they would whisper
How my life would always be a complete disgrace

No matter where I turned on my journey
To escape so many years of frustration
I struggled from one storm to the next trying
To find the cure for my broken heart's desolation

Through all my long days and sleepless nights
Of trying to make sense of it all
I prayed God would send me a spiritual friend
To love me through all my faults

After many years of making bad choices
And trusting my heart with the wrong souls
I met a hummingbird watching me from the trees
Above with such admiration that I could not let go

I had so many tears in my eyes from all
The hurts my life had brought me

Yet the way this little hummingbird looked at me
Could heal all my pain and cure my deepest misery

He flapped his little wings at me
With such elegance and grace
I felt God sent this sweet bird to me as a new friend
Who would love me in the greatest ways

As our eyes met, I felt a connection
Unlike anything I had ever had
Somehow the calm way this little bird looked
Into my soul made my weary heart feel less sad

I was not sure why I had to meet this
Little hummingbird so late in my life
Yet as I kept walking my path he flew gently
Above me making sure I felt strong and all right

In times of great rain and moments when it felt
The harsh winds of change would never cease
All I had to do was look above me and see
My new little friend flying to keep my spirit in peace

I could have the worst days of my life yet know
The hummingbird would always be my friend
We had a special language without words
And a magical love between us that will never end

Through all my ups and downs and times
When life is full of unclear reasons

I just think of my special friend the hummingbird
Who protects me through all life's seasons

Chapter 9 - An Agape Kind of Love

Magical Message #9 – Remember that true love gives without expecting anything in return.

The beauty of love lies within the heart and soul of someone who truly gives of himself without expecting anything in return. In this world, so many people treat love as if it is dependent on what others can do for us when in all actuality, it should be more about what we can do for those we love. I have found that the most pure and genuine kind of love is that which comes from God. It is an agape kind of love that is built on the most unconditional nature. This is the type of love that never leaves us or fails us. It remains the type of love that helps us overcome our battles and embrace the triumphs of life. With an agape kind of love, God can transform our hearts and souls in the most beautiful ways possible.

I have been healed and both hurt by love, but the one kind of love that has never hurt me is the spiritual love God always has for me. If we are all lucky, there may come a time that God leads us to a soul mate of sorts that feels an agape love for us. A soul mate connection is one that is based on a love that is eternal, where two hearts are connected as one, a connection where the very essence of true love becomes the breath and life of the one with whom God has meant for us to stay bonded.

The following poem, "An Agape Kind of Love", is a true reflection of the nature of unconditional, spiritual love that lasts forever.

An Agape Kind of Love

I was feeling lost and confused
About the nature of love
In my many questions I asked God
How do you know when it is real and from above

He just sent a few raindrops my way
To say how does the rain make you feel
I said a little bit down and yet though things are gloomy
Maybe I can find a love that is always real

I tried and tried to understand why everywhere
I turned looked dark and dreary

I said God how can I find the love I really need
When I just feel so weak and weary

God just looked right down at me
With eyes full of great wit
He sent a rainbow after the storm to remind me
There is a colorful love in life that never will quit

I was still confused and not sure
Why love seemed always out of my reach
I asked God to give me some inner strength
Or send something my way with a lesson to teach

God then looked down and sent some snow my way
That felt peaceful to my troubled soul
Then I realized when I focused on the serenity of it
I could finally let some of my craziness go

I still could not figure out why everyone else
Seemed to be so happy on the outside
Then God said if you look a little deeper
So many are crying for a real love on the inside

In all my searching and wondering
How do you know when love is right and true
God said around you is an unconditional love
Through a kindred soul who is always there for you

Still trying to understand exactly what
God meant for me to really find

MAGICAL LOVE MESSAGES BETWEEN KINDRED SPIRITS

I noticed a little red bird perched on a tree
Flapping its wings just to say I'm here for you all the time

With a smile on my face and a determination
To really feel a love that I could truly embrace
I looked in front of me and caught a vision of a calm lake
Reassuring me its water would keep me safe

As I walked a little further down this path
Trying to find a love that was so right
In the night I saw the stars dancing with the moon
Just so I would know everything would be all right

With intrigue in my heart I was so curious
What else God wanted me to see
Then I noticed a beautiful sunset over a mountain top
Letting me know I would conquer my misery

I was so amazed at all the things I had been shown
And wondered what was next in store
Then I saw angels reaching out to me as if to say
Keep the faith and you will be blessed with more

I kept walking my path and wondered
Why I never noticed it until now
I could feel the gentle energy of a loving presence
Giving me hope I would make it somehow

As I came to the edge of a cliff that marked the
End of the curious path upon which I walked

I thanked God for showing me that true love
Exists in the silent beauty of nature's finest thoughts

I held my hand close over my heart and asked God
To help me keep this agape love that never died
He just whispered your soul mate was in every
Act of nature you saw to love you and be your guide

I was finally happy after all my struggles and searching
For the key to a love that would last forever
God sent a gentle breeze and a warmer spirit
Through my soul mate's love that I would always treasure

Chapter 10 - An Enchanting Tale Between Two Kindred Souls

Magical Message #10 – Sometimes we all need to dream of a love that will always protect us.

I have learned that sometimes in life we will all experience moments when we need to feel a connection to a love like no other. Connections in this life are powerful, and sometimes they can be even more powerful when we feel a longing to something deeper, something that transforms the entire ways we look at and think about our lives.

Finding a true heartfelt connection is a challenge for most people whether it be a good friendship or a romantic partner. Being able to connect with another soul that knows you better than you even know yourself is even a greater struggle for so many of us. However, do not lose heart because spiritual connections that are unique are also the very ones we must embrace when times are tough and even when life is full of joyous occasions.

The following poem, "An Enchanting Tale Between Two Kindred Souls", is a fairy tale of sorts that illustrates the simple beauty of a spiritual connection, and yet an even deeper reflection of a forever love destined to last for eternity. This poem reflects the various past lives two kindred spirits have shared and the love that remained alive between them.

An Enchanting Tale Between Two Kindred Souls

I can feel a mystic pull between one half of my soul
To someone who knows me well
It is like we were bound to love each other forever
Where we always had a unique story to tell

In one life we were family sharing
Secrets along life's way
In another life we were lovers meant to share
The depths of our heart's up and downs everyday

In one life we took vows to love each other
Through the best and worst of times
Even when the world seemed tough, the love we shared
Could survive chaos and unhealthy signs

In one life you were my partner through
Every moment that passed

MAGICAL LOVE MESSAGES BETWEEN KINDRED SPIRITS

In the next life you were the one holding my heart
When my body was too weak to last

In one season we shared words of a great story
Only you and I could understand
No matter how hard the world could be
You were the one always holding my hand

Sometimes the days were so cold I did not think
I could ever stay warm from the chilly air
Yet you always wrapped your loving arms around me
So I would know you would always be there

In one life I felt I was lost and
Had nobody by my side
Yet you surrounded me by your magnetic energy
As if to say I will be with you all the time

In one season I felt like I just wanted to give up
Because my life seemed so wrong
But in the midst of my despair you had a way of
Whispering have faith and always stay strong

In some lives I lived I can remember that
So many people let me down
When you looked at me I could feel our love was
Powerful enough to turn my smile into a frown

There were sometimes I wondered why
So many others tried to keep us apart

HEATHER D. WRIGHT

Yet in the midst of a lonely night, I could feel you
By my side keeping me safe through the dark

In so many areas of our lives I know that
You have never really left me alone
Through the light and dark of each day
You have always been the place my heart has called home

In times of sadness there have been many lives
Where I felt all I could do was cry
Yet you could gently wipe away the tears
Because you felt my pain and all those curious whys

From one life to the next and through the
Seasons of winter, spring, summer, and fall
I know the love that binds our souls together is
The force that keeps us strong and able to stand tall

Through every life we have lived until now
We often feel a pull that is often hard for us to discuss
We continue to share a language of a sacred love that is
Built on unconditional hope and mutual trust

Chapter 11 – An Unbreakable Connection Between Twin Souls

Magical Message #11 – Never underestimate the powerful bond that exists between heartfelt connections.

There are some connections in life that I feel God has destined for us to embrace. Many connections I feel are spiritual. In life there will be some people we feel totally drawn to. It could be a family member, a close friend, or a lover. No matter what the nature of the connection, a twin soul relationship is based on unconditional love. When God created Adam and Eve, I feel they were twin souls, two people who shared the same soul between each other.

In the same way, I feel God has destined for us all to feel a special connection to someone that is unlike anything we have ever felt with anyone else. A twin soul connection is powerful and unbreakable. With these connections, twin souls can feel each others' emotions. They know exactly when the other half of their soul is feeling great and exactly when the other half of their soul is hurting. Their connection is based on a love that can never end because a twin soul connection is eternal. Being in the same place at the same time for twin souls is like living in a true paradise, and when they are apart it can be the hardest struggle for them.

The following poem, "An Unbreakable Connection Between Twin Souls", discusses the nature of a twin soul connection as well as how two like minded souls are able to use their connection to help each other through the good and bad times of life.

An Unbreakable Connection Between Twin Souls

I can whisper your name and you
Always seem to come to my side
It is like we lived lifetimes together
With an unbreakable love that kept us able to survive

There were times I did not think I could
Make it without your sweet touch
I can remember in each lifetime
You were the one who loved me so much

There was a tie between us that

MAGICAL LOVE MESSAGES BETWEEN KINDRED SPIRITS

Nobody ever seemed to break
It was like nobody could understand the
Connection that helped us through all of our mistakes

Every now and then I get a feeling of how
Your heart used to be so close to mine
In every season we shared the air
We breathed as if we were frozen in time

I can recall all the moments that
You just held my weary hand
In times of sadness, you comforted my grieving soul
Letting me know you would always understand

When life seemed so hard that it just
Was too much for me to bear
You were always the one with such faith in me
And a heart that would forever care

There were so many lifetimes I feel we lived
That somehow I just cannot forget
It seemed that through every lesson we learned
You were the soul helping me never lose my creative step

In this lifetime I feel a connection
To you that is magical and true
No matter how crazy life gets I know that
I will always feel a special love for you

My heart feels in sync with your spirit

HEATHER D. WRIGHT

From the moment we met so many lifetimes ago
All I have to do is think of you and know
You have the key to my half complete soul

Sometimes I send you energy just so you know
I love you with all of my heart
I am weak on the outside but our spiritual connection
Has kept us together right from the start

Through times of life's hardest
Trials and tribulations
You were the one giving without question
And with heartfelt revelations

I can reach for you and feel that
You have a way of reaching for me
You just seem to know how to comfort
My sadness and rescue me from misery

In the dark of night I have a dream of
Just being close to you without any fear
I can feel you reach within my soul and
Whisper the right words that wipes away all my tears

No matter where a dream takes us or
Where the journey of this life leads us
You will always be the breath of hope
That keeps my heart from being so restless

Chapter 12 - Finding Refuge in a Soulmate's Heart

Magical Message #12 – Trust that there are people who will love you no matter what happens.

In life it is often hard to face each day not knowing exactly what to expect and even less not knowing if we can walk the path alone. I do believe in the concept of soulmates. In fact, this connection could be a family member, a good friend, a co-worker, a role model, a romantic partner, or even a pet. No matter what the nature of the relationship, soulmates have a connection that makes them feel truly complete and loved whether they are in the presence of their loved one or not. When you have a soulmate connection, you will feel a strong pull in your heart to be around that person. It could be that you are meant to learn a lesson, but I feel more than anything it is meant for you to feel a close connection and love unlike no other.

The following poem, "Finding Refuge in a Soulmate's Heart", is a story of one soul who has found a connection with someone he can trust. On his best and worst days, he knows that he can have faith God has put someone special in his life whose mere presence makes him feel truly loved and protected at all times. In a world where others often get taken for granted, true soulmates learn to value their connection and help each other through all the seasons of life. Through love and sacrifice, they learn to never let go of each other and to trust that their connection is everlasting.

Finding Refuge in a Soulmate's Heart

I was losing my mind
Feeling I had no control
All I wanted was everyone to leave me alone
So I could find you and hold you close

I felt nothing made sense and all the voices
Of endless chatter disrupted my mind
All I really needed was to hear the echo of your voice
To keep me focused on the present time

I did not know how to break away from
The people talking so loudly here and there

MAGICAL LOVE MESSAGES BETWEEN KINDRED SPIRITS

All I wanted to do was focus on you because
I need you to know I will always care

I felt like I was struggling in a sea of confusion
To find my way out my distress
When I just need to feel at ease I long for
A glimpse of you to put my weary soul at rest

I sometimes feel that the whole world is crazy
And you are the only one that puts me at ease
No matter how everyone else gets you are
The one my heart clings to in forever peace

I often cannot find the words to tell you
What I really do think and feel
But I feel an energy between us that tells of
A forever love story that for us will always be real

Every day that passes I often
Wonder how you are
Through the good and bad days of my life
I know you will always be my brightest star

I can be in the most crowded room and feel
As if nobody really understands me at all
Then I get a sweet vision of you reaching to comfort me
With your special smile to keep me calm

Some days I am not sure if I am going to be able
To survive without looking right into your eyes

Yet somehow the connection I feel to you gives me
The vision I need to make it through the night

I know life is hard and it seems there are
Always obstacles standing in our way
But I know deep within the spiritual tie that links us
Keeps us connected and out of harm's way

I often think of you and hope that life
Is giving you the best you desire
No matter where I am I know I love you with
Such a passion within that is as strong as a raging fire

If only you could see on the inside
Just how much I truly adore your soul
Then you would know you can rest assured
I love you too much to ever let you go

I feel you around me when I really
Need a special, loving friend
It's like I can feel totally lost
And yet the thoughts of you renew my strength within

Even though life can be very hard
Making it tough for us to stand strong
I can embrace the energy that binds
Our souls together by the most divine love song

MAGICAL LOVE MESSAGES BETWEEN KINDRED SPIRITS

Chapter 13 - I Love the Way

Magical Message #13 – Don't ever doubt the power of love to transform your life.

I have often felt so down sometimes that I truly wondered if I was ever going to make it to the next day. In fact, I questioned how I could ever endure my constant hardships and yet come out stronger on the other side. It is in moments like this that I truly feel God shows us He loves us through the presence of someone we trust and with whom we feel close. In a world full of negative people, it seems there are not that many authentic people out there anymore. When you do find a trustworthy soul that understands you and has a way of helping you through your struggles, do not let him or her go.

The following poem, "I Love the Way", is a poetic love letter of sorts from one soul to another thanking the person he has come to cherish for touching his life. It is the kind of poem that hopefully will inspire all of us that life is so short and we should take the time to thank someone for the positive difference he or she has made in our lives. This poem is a creative way of telling someone special just how much you love him or her for enriching your life.

I Love the Way

I love the way you can walk into a room
And light up the darkness that tries to break me down
Despite my struggles your gentle presence
Soothes my restless soul with the most peaceful sound

I love the way you can bring positive energy
Into my spirit that sometimes feels lifeless and alone
The way you look at me calms my fears and provides
A safe journey for me to find my way home

I love the way you can catch the world on fire
With your enthusiastic spirit that never dies
In times of chaos you remain the trustworthy soul
That helps me see through the world's lies

I love the way you can send me healing energy
When it seems nothing else feels right
After a time in your presence I have a serene feeling within
That helps me sleep softly at night

I love the way you can send me a message that
You care so much through your magnetic charm
No matter how good or bad my days may be
You are my refuge of hope keeping me safe from harm

I love the way your eyes greet me
As if to say you truly understand
Your warm spirit gives me hope like a lost soul
Needing direction who takes God by the hand

I love the way I can walk past you when you smile at me
With an energy that communicates much
In the midst of my trying times and long journeys
My soul feels your loving, creative touch

I love the way you can sense when things in my world
Seem destructive and unbalanced
Somehow you play the right song that sends a calm energy
To protect me from the world's malice

I love the way you can tell when I am
Feeling the very best I can be
When our positive energies collide we can
Set the world on fire with our spiritual chemistry

I love the way I can be either near or far away from you
In the same place and you pull me close
We share a silent language of kinship and trust
That only we are privileged to know

MAGICAL LOVE MESSAGES BETWEEN KINDRED SPIRITS

I love the way you connect with me when
I am away from you in another time and place
Even in the midst of a busy day or among other people
I can feel your caring and honest ways

I love the way I can take a walk outside
And experience nature's beauty at its best
Somehow I feel it is your way of sending me
Encouraging energy to get some much needed rest

I love the way I can be listening to the radio
When I hear a familiar song
In that moment I feel you encouraging me to stay happy
And to know the bad times won't last long

I love the way I can escape to the online world
That provides a different type of connection
I can see the positive things you post and know that
With you I don't have to worry about rejection

I love the way I can be lost in a dream
During the course of any night
As I sleep, I can feel your loving energy preparing me
To face a new day ahead with love and light

I love the way I can feel your energies
No matter where either of us may be
All I know is I can rest assured you will
Never leave my side no matter what the tragedy

I love the way you have shown me what
True spiritual love means to deeply feel
I just want to thank God for allowing us
To be kindred spirits connected by a love that is real

Chapter 14 - Magical Ties Through Mystical Times

Magical Message #14 – Trust in what you feel to be real to give you strength.

I have always loved magic, and I really believe that life can be one great magical journey. God gave us a destiny, and we must learn that with the good comes the bad. However, even when we feel depressed and as if life is trying to break us apart, we must look around and trust that God sends us signs to help us. When we feel connections to nature that we cannot explain, then we must trust what we feel. In essence, we must trust that the pull we feel to certain things God has created hold hidden wisdom we are meant to uncover.

The following poem, "Magical Ties through Mystical Times", tells an interesting story of one soul who feels alone and broken. It is as if he has come to the end of his rope feeling desperate for change and even more eager for something to help heal his wounded soul. Through the meeting with a magical flower, this soul realizes that God has put this flower in his path to give him courage and renewed strength that he can face anything in life.

Magical Ties through Mystical Times

I was leaning in a direction not so sure
Of the path where I wanted to go
Somewhere in the corner of my mind I could feel
Destiny pulling on my much hungry soul

I was not sure what to do or where to look
For the answers I so needed for my mind
All I could feel was my restless spirit was tired
Of hitting brick walls leaving me running out of time

On a bright, sunny day when it seemed the sunshine
Would keep me warm and feeling strong
I decided to walk along a path full of fresh red roses
That seemed to sing a beautiful love song

When I listened a little more closely it was as if
There was one that carried a special connection
So I plucked it from the ground holding it close
To my needy heart feeling lost in a sea of rejection

I could smell a sweet fragrance from this little red rose

MAGICAL LOVE MESSAGES BETWEEN KINDRED SPIRITS

Filling my weary spirit with much hope
Somehow there was some aura around its strong stem
Giving me the strength to always cope

I walked a little further and noticed the path
Where I walked was not as sunny or clear as before
I kept stumbling on the rocks in my way that seemed
As if they were draining my energies forevermore

With much confusion and a curious desire
That maybe I should turn back
A delicate rose petal fell on my feet with a soft touch
Helping me realize I was on the right track

As the days grew long and
The nights much deeper
I felt another rose petal caress my hand
With a warm feeling that my life would get easier

Not sure of why this special rose and I seemed
So close as if nobody could tear us apart
Somewhere in the depths of my soul he seemed
To carry the key to my much desiring heart

Through the rain and storms when
Each of his petals seemed to wither
My tears would meet the dew on his stems
Bringing our needy souls much closer together

I could see one by one that each of his rose petals

Were falling as we endured the fall and winter days
Yet I collected the petals and carried them in my pocket
For courage to endure life's crazy ways

I remember hoping that one day my friend the rose
Would blossom with great joy once again
Yet while holding it without its lovely petals
I could feel its strength never leave me like a true friend

As the cold days ended and the sun was shining
On the dreary trail where I was meant to travel
I could see the rose petals blooming again healing
My wounded soul from life's treacherous battles

I finally made my way home to the place
Where life seemed to make sense
When I held my friend the rose close to my heart
I knew his love had inspired me to never quit

It is funny how every year despite when its petals fall
This admirable red rose never dies
When I carry my friend, the connection we share
Remains a timeless love story that always feels right

Chapter 15 - My Soul Cat and Me

———

Magical Message #15: Sometimes a beloved pet can be a trusted companion and a very best friend.

When it comes to trusted companions, I truly feel animals are God's gift to our hearts and souls. I have always loved animals from the time I was child, and I spent much of my life with either a cat or dog in my presence.

Of all the pets I ever had, there was one special cat named Jasper that I got when I was in college. I have to admit that the first time I saw Jasper I knew she was different. It was as if she connected right to my soul with the strong ways she would look into my eyes. I would often carry her over my shoulder, and she would lay next to me no matter where I was or what I did. She became my true friend in ways I could not explain. It was if she could sense when I was happy, sad, or just downright frustrated with my continual efforts to feel my best despite the odds that were often against me.

I guess you could say Jasper became what I call my soul cat because I never loved another animal in my life the way I loved her. I had Jasper for 16 years, and when she got sick, I let her go in peace reading her some of my most comforting poems as she crossed over to Rainbow Bridge, the place where animals enjoy the afterlife. I knew I had lost my best friend but more than that, my soul friend. Even though Jasper is no longer with me in the physical realm, I feel her spiritually beside me often. The following poem, "My Soul Cat and Me" is a reflection of the connection and life I shared with my dear friend, Jasper. I hope this poem serves as a comforting force for anyone who has loved and lost a pet as animals really do hold a special place in our hearts.

My Soul Cat and Me

I was driving down the road
Wondering what I should do
Then I looked into the seat beside me
And saw a glimpse of you

You were a cute little black and white kitten
That really caught my eye
Somehow I knew you wanted me to feel
You could take my life by a special kind of surprise

MAGICAL LOVE MESSAGES BETWEEN KINDRED SPIRITS

I looked into your face wondering
If you wanted me to take you home
You just meowed softly as if to say
I am always going to be connected to your soul

During my mid to late twenties
You and I would often play together
I would go hide and you would seek me out
No matter what the crazy weather

In times when the days were bright and sunny
I would take you outside to play
You just jumped on to my lap as I sat in the grass
Taking a break from life's crazy ways

As I got a little older feeling pulled
In so many difficult directions
I could feel you walk across my feet
As if to say I will always offer you protection

Every now and then when I needed
A very good friend to call my own
All I had to do was hold you close to my heart
And feel you purr letting me know I was not alone

During the later years in my life when time
Seemed to create less time for us to be together
All I had to do was just think of you
And know we were connected always and forever

I can still remember all the late nights
I could not sleep and you would be there
All I had to do was carry you over my shoulder
Knowing you would always care

Many days and nights have passed and you
Never let a moment pass without sitting by my side
You sensed the deeper sadness within me
That nobody ever understood without asking why

As the years have passed and as time
Passed on between us
I noticed you grew a little weaker
But I refused to lose sight of our bond of trust

In my heart I knew that at some point
Your life was destined to come to an end
I just kept hoping that God would let you live
As long as possible as my soul connected friend

Despite my hopes that you would grow strong again
I could sense your body was getting weaker
I watched your once courageous body grow faint
As you continued getting sicker

In the last few days of your life
I did my best to spend as much time with you as I could
Somehow I knew the time had come for me to let you go
Although it did not make me feel so good

MAGICAL LOVE MESSAGES BETWEEN KINDRED SPIRITS

As you struggled to keep fighting to survive
I felt you wanted to please me no matter what
I prayed to God to give you either the courage to live
Or strength to die before my heart stopped

When you took your last few breaths
I was not sure if I could really let you go
Now that you have crossed over to Rainbow Bridge
I still feel the great love always uniting our souls

Chapter 16 - The Butterfly that Became My Friend

Magical Message #16: Never take a good friend for granted.

As I reflect back upon my life, I can honestly say I have had my ups and downs in the area of friendship. I always was so quick to trust others even when my intuition was encouraging me to be on guard. For all the times I did not listen to my instincts, I found myself in a world of hurt from thinking someone was a true friend when that was just not the case.

Despite the disappointments I have had in the area of friendship, God has also blessed me with some very beautiful friends. I truly feel there are some friends that God sends into our lives that are like soulmates because they resonate with our own spirits during the best and worst of times.

The following poem, "The Butterfly that Became My
Friend", is a story about a lost soul who feels nobody
understands him, and he is longing to find a true friend
with whom he can relate. It is a special narrative poem
about two souls being drawn together by the true divine
intervention of God knowing that they were meant to
cross paths and help each other along the way.

The Butterfly that Became My Friend

On a warm, sunny day
In the midst of spring
A little, orange butterfly came flying down
A nature trail in search of me

For some reason it seemed
To want to stay right by my side
The way it was drawn to me felt like
A lost friend I missed from another life

I thought maybe I should just quit feeling
I was unworthy of the little black butterfly's attention
The more intrigued I became with him
The more I sensed he had the best of intentions

I watched him briefly as he sat
On a flower right beside my path
His aura was so peaceful that he made me feel
I no longer had to keep looking back

When I walked a little further down this trail
That had become my escape from my distress
As I lost my balance the little orange butterfly flapped
Its wings in front of me to put my soul at rest

The more I walked the little orange butterfly
Embraced other flowers that touched me with their grace
Somehow the special ways he embraced each flower
Made me feel I could trust his caring ways

After feeling like I had endured so many trials
That almost kept me feeling down
I felt this little orange butterfly had been my truest friend
In many lives including this town

Feeling that maybe I was meant to cross paths
With this unique butterfly I had come to adore
He flew right in front of me with such elegance
And I felt drawn to his charm even more

He had this magical way of never
Being really out of my sight
I could feel he wanted me to know how devoted
He was to making sure I was feeling all right

In a matter of time the little orange butterfly and I
Seemed to develop a special kind of connection
We were linked with such love and trust that
We looked out for one another with great protection

MAGICAL LOVE MESSAGES BETWEEN KINDRED SPIRITS

All I had to do was have faith in my newest friend
That came to brighten up my heart
When I needed to know someone really loved me
I knew the orange butterfly would not let me fall apart

Chapter 17 - The Coloring Box of Love

Magical Message #17: Just as there are many colorful crayons, there are many shades of love to experience.

I have always been fascinated by what I would like to call the crayola box syndrome which is the way I perceive how different colors convey diverse meanings. After reflecting on the different colors of crayons that exist, I thought how using the strokes of various colors could express unique expressions of love.

The following poem, "The Coloring Box of Love", is all about how each color in this magical box of diversity paints a special piece of the puzzle about love and how it can create miracles in many special situations.

In this life I feel it would be great if our whole world was one coloring box of love because there are many ways to

express such sentiments no matter what flavor of the
crayon is used.

The Coloring Box of Love

I bought a box of crayons hoping
To color a new picture just for me
Something inside my soul said
Draw several hearts and color them wisely

I grabbed an orange crayon to draw
A heart filled with optimism and grace
My soul said this is where love could lead
When you let go of pessimistic ways

I then reached for a green crayon to draw
A heart that was balanced and fully grown
My sixth sense said trust that the
Right love will lead your heart to its hopeful home

I picked up a blue crayon to draw
A heart that was peaceful and true
My mind said the right love
You need will always be loyal to you

I took a purple crayon and drew a heart
That was full of great intuition
The spiritual side of my soul said
Real love will help you see past all the superstition

I found a brown crayon to create a heart
That was friendly and down-to-earth
An angelic voice whispered the best kind
Of love helps you appreciate your self-worth

I discovered a gray crayon to help me
Draw a heart that was willing to compromise
My gut feeling encouraged me that a
Trustworthy love never hides behind deceptive lies

I stumbled across a gold crayon to help me
Draw a heart that was honest and victorious
I knew God showed me the best love appreciates
You and makes you feel simply glorious

I decided to take a chance on a black crayon
To draw a heart that was full of mystery
Inside myself I knew the most meaningful
Kind of love would satisfy my curiosity

I made a special effort to use a white crayon
To draw a heart that was innocent and pure
Its comforting aura made me feel agape love
Was the kind of love of which I could be truly sure

Then I decided to take the pink and red crayons
And draw the biggest heart I could ever find
In that moment God whispered unconditional love
Is where you will embrace real happiness this time

Chapter 18 - The Comforting Scratch on the Door

Magical Message #18: Friendly spirits such as our pets comfort us when we need it most.

In a previous chapter, I shared a story and poem about my dear cat, Jasper, who passed away a few years ago. As I shared earlier, Jasper and I had a very special connection. Not too long after Jasper died, I was visiting the home of my parents where Jasper lived all her life. Late one night in the beginning of the fall before I went to bed, I heard a scratch on the basement door that sounded like Jasper when she wanted to come into the living room from downstairs.

Now I knew Jasper had died, and at this point, my mother had not gotten a new cat. However, the scratch on the basement door sounded so real. Prior to hearing this sound I was feeling very distraught and sad over Jasper's loss feeling as if I had truly lost my best friend. I was feeling down about my career and personal matters, and in some way I was longing to feel my cat's presence, which is why I felt what I witnessed was so real.

The following poem, "The Comforting Scratch on the Door", is my reflection on this experience and how it helped me. I truly believe the spirits of pets we have loved and lost can come back to visit us even after they have crossed over to the Rainbow Bridge. Just as we can feel the spirit of any loved one who has crossed over, I feel animals have a special way of connecting to their owners left behind just to let us know their spirit is always with us.

To this day, I have many pictures of my long lost cat in many places in my home. Her memory and spirit lives on in my heart and soul just as the energy from any animal you have loved and lost will remain by your side in every avenue of life.

The Comforting Scratch on the Door

Late at night when I was
Trying to relax and all
I heard a faint scratch on my door that appeared
Out of the blue at the beginning of fall

Amazed and wondering if it was my

MAGICAL LOVE MESSAGES BETWEEN KINDRED SPIRITS

Long lost cat who was coming to visit
All I could feel was this was a magical time
To explore something most exquisite

Not sure if I should open the door
For fear my dear friend may not be around
In my heart I felt she wanted me to know
Her spirit would never leave my own peaceful town

Wondering in some way if she was trying
To send me a message to keep trying as hard as I can
Despite the craziness of my life I felt in my most
Trying moments she did truly understand

The more I listened to this faint scratch
I knew there had to be a reason
The energies of the cat I called friend knew
How to give me hope no matter what the season

I reflected back to the past to the times
My furry friend would just sit in my lap
Even when I felt too tired to keep going
I could feel her comforting my fears with a serene nap

I smiled knowing that I would never really be
Alone without the friend who loved me so much
Through the scratch on my door I could feel
The warmth of her paws love me with the sweetest touch

Chapter 19 - The Day Fear Took a Chance on Love

―――――――

Magical Message #19: Sometimes we have to be willing to overcome our fears to embrace the power of love.

I really do think fear is one of the hardest emotions to face and even more difficult to overcome. We all have fears I feel of the things that we seem to desire most. In my experience, I feel what most people fear is getting real with the needs of their own heart. It is easier at times to play it safe when it would be best to follow the divine guidance of where we are meant to be.

I know this well because I have been hurt quite often in matters of the heart, but I learned that no matter how much I may have gotten hurt, I should always keep my heart open to all the many different forms of love that exist in this world.

MAGICAL LOVE MESSAGES BETWEEN KINDRED SPIRITS

The following poem, "The Day Fear Took a Chance on Love", is all about learning from past relationship mistakes and finding the courage and strength to move on to a better place where the beauty of real love exists. It is a poem about finding the chance to love again despite the difficult circumstances of life knowing that through the fears we face that true love is there waiting for us.

The Day Fear Took a Chance on Love

I was so afraid of
Taking another chance
I thought what if I fail and lose again
To another unfortunate circumstance

I did not think I could ever catch my breath
After all the losses where I felt used
I just needed something to bring me back to life again
So I would not feel so hopeless and abused

I spent a lot of time thinking it would be best
If I just continued to play it safe
I felt if I took a risk I may look like a romantic fool
With a heart that had been disgraced

I was feeling like I was not meant
To be on the lucky side of life
I could feel the pain of lost love
Haunting my memories and keeping me up at night

I knew I had kept my heart in chains
Since all of my heartbreaks
I just thought what if I trust too much
And risk making more inevitable mistakes

I looked around for God to give me a sign
That could lead me to a love that could last forever
I just was afraid when I found it
My wounded soul would still be broken and severed

I was not too sure if love would even
Want someone like me in its midst
I thought I had lost the opportunity to embrace
A new love because of all my past impulsive risks

I decided that maybe God had a lesson
That He really needed for me to learn
I discovered that true spiritual love would
Never leave me feeling cheated nor deeply burned

I realized that I was not like all
Of my family and dear friends
I was meant to escape this life and live
In the spirit world where unconditional love never ends

I closed my eyes and asked God to take me
Into that magical place where I could not get hurt
I asked Him to help me feel the kind of love
That never fails or leaves us feeling lower than dirt

MAGICAL LOVE MESSAGES BETWEEN KINDRED SPIRITS

I found myself in a new world where others
Were not afraid to truly love and enjoy their fate
I could finally put my restless soul at ease knowing
That my heart finally found a safe place to stay

Chapter 20 - The Day Sad Fell in Love With Happy

Magical Message #20: What once was sad can become a happy experience with love and patience.

Sometimes we all just feel really sad at times wondering how many setbacks we have to endure before our lives are at the place we want them to be. It is human nature to grow unhappy and depressed when it feels our world is crumbling before our eyes. In times of great despair, we wonder if we will ever overcome the sadness we feel just for a chance to embrace the true spirit of happiness.

In the following poem, "The Day Sad Fell in Love with Happy", you will discover a story about a lost soul named Sad who is truly at the verge of giving up in his life. He feels he has nothing meaningful to look forward to until after he meets a new friend whose name is Happy. Once

----

Sad Meets Happy, she helps Sad realize he is not all alone
and that she is there to help him no matter what.

As you read this poem, you will feel the struggles of
sadness followed by the beauty and grace of true happiness
in its most beautiful form. This poem is about realizing
that even through and after our sadness, brighter and
happier days remain right around the corner.

The Day Sad Fell in Love with Happy

Once upon a time
There was broken soul named Sad
He felt nobody ever understood him
And always wanted to make him mad

At times Sad wondered how long it would be
Before he would find a true friend
Yet no matter how hard he tried
It seemed his misery would never come to an end

In times of hardship
And in times of much great pain
Sad thought maybe he should give up
On ever finding love and overcoming his past shame

Somehow in the depths of his soul
Sad knew that life was all about hanging in there
Even when others broke his heart he had to trust
That there was someone out there who did care

Sad searched through every corner around him
For a chance to find some reason to smile
He knew there had to be someone to love him
For his true self and make him feel worthwhile

When all the long nights and weeks passed
With nobody to caress his struggling heart
Sad just kept on wondering when he would get
A chance to find a fresh, new start

Then one day out of the clear air it seemed
All Sad's darkness was broken by a bright light
He looked around to see why suddenly his world
Seemed a little more than just a long, dark night

Then an angelic presence cast a new vision
That was creative and bold
Sad was greeted by this new divine presence
Bringing warmth to his spirit that had grown cold

The angelic spirit walked up to Sad
And she held her arms out so wide
She said her name was Happy and she had come
To help Sad feel better this time

With a look of confusion Sad was not quite sure
How Happy could set him free
Yet somehow he trusted his instincts
That this encounter was meant to be

MAGICAL LOVE MESSAGES BETWEEN KINDRED SPIRITS

After Happy gave Sad the warmest embrace
He had ever felt in his existence
Sad knew he had finally met a spiritual force
That could help him overcome all his past resistance

Happy took her hand and touched Sad's face
As if she knew he had been waiting for a chance
Sad could feel the passion of a love he had wanted
But never found due to lost circumstance

Happy wiped the tears streaming down from Sad's face
So he would know all would be well
Through every tear of pain Sad cried
Happy knew that his broken heart had many stories to tell

Happy looked Sad in the eyes with a powerful look of love
That was truly out of this world
Sad knew within himself that Happy wanted
To heal his wounds and help him overcome his turmoil

Happy reached for Sad's hand and said
I want you to come follow me
She reassured him that their meeting was truly
A divine intervention of romantic destiny

Even though Sad was still healing from years
Of being broken and confused
Somehow walking hand in hand with Happy
On a new path was like a dream of hope come true

On this new path upon which Sad and Happy
Walked so closely together
They both knew there would be times
They would have to endure both good and bad weather

Yet as they kept walking they knew that
There was a bond of love keeping their souls in sync
Despite the ups and downs of life
Sad and Happy always trusted in love and their instincts

Chapter 21 - The Deep Breath Between Soulmates

Magical Message #21: There are some forms of love that can be conditional based on what others expect of us, but there is a deeper love that exists between soulmates that keeps the very depth of their souls alive and strong.

Love is a powerful force that so many people want to feel, yet so many people place conditions on how they love someone else based on what that person can do for us or be for us. Some people want us to love them based on certain conditions because it suits their needs at the time.

However, there is an unconditional love that exists between soulmates which is one that is able to withstand the test of time and last for eternity. With true soul mates, love is always strong, and it can endure the toughest problems. Even when others try to tear it apart, this love is powerful, and it will never fail those whose hearts have been blessed to receive it.

The following poem, "The Deep Breath Between Soulmates", is a breathtaking journey into the heartfelt connection that two like-minded souls share.

The Deep Breath Between Soulmates

I can feel you breathe into me
As I breathe into you
Somehow destiny has linked us together
By a spiritual love that is forever true

When I stand alone I find that I am suffocating
In a world where I have always felt mistaken
Then you come my way
And I realize you are the one helping me feel awakened

I can drown myself in the air you breathe
As if it speaks to my inner soul
There is a peace within your spirit holding onto me
So I never can let you go

I can be pulled in every way you can imagine
And feel nobody understands
Then I feel the magical touch of your breath
Into my world and the warmth of your caring hands

There are times I wonder if I can ever make it through

MAGICAL LOVE MESSAGES BETWEEN KINDRED SPIRITS

A day without your magical touch
I know in my heart there has never been another
I have loved so much

Everyday I feel I am being tossed about
By a wind that tries to break me down
Then I can hear the air you breathe
As if you are the calm voice in a mix of crazy sounds

Day in and day out I feel that I am
Running so wildly I do not know how to stop
Sometimes within my lonely soul I feel you are
The anchor that keeps me from blowing my top

It seems I can talk a thousand words over
And yet nobody really hears what I say
Then I can share the air we breathe in a crowded room
And feel your energy that all will be ok

In times of separation when I feel lost
Without you by my side
I can take a deep breath and feel all the despair
Within is replaced by your love that is one of a kind

When I take a walk in nature I can feel you
Reach for me through the cool, crisp air
Then as I take a deep breath
I can feel your energy speak to me that you will always care

I can lie awake at night and feel the anxiety

Of not being near you scare my mind
Then I embrace the air of the night
Escaping into a dream where I can be with you all the time

Some nights I do not sleep well because
I think of how much I miss your loving connection
When the air I breathe is full of such pain
You are the one who frees me from daily deception

I can feel you breathe into me as I breathe
Into you every day and every night
I can feel the depth of our connection
Is the star that guides our hearts with the brightest light

I can feel you breathe into me as I breathe into you
With every breath destiny gives us
Know in my heart we are linked with a spiritual love
Keeping us in sync with forever trust

Chapter 22 - The Enduring Spirit of Love Through Nine Lives

Magical Message #22: Love is the force that carries us through so many lifetimes, and it is through each lifetime, that we learn about the power of love and its ability to give us strength in our weakest moments.

I have always felt that love is the one powerful force in this life that carries us through so many changes. In fact, I feel that we have all lived many different lives and through each one we have learned just how powerful love can truly be. No matter how many lives we have lived, the one force I feel that endures is love. Through every chapter of life we experience, I feel love shapes our hopes and dreams in many special ways.

The following poem, "An Enduring Love through Nine Lives", is taken from the idea of how cats are known for living nine lives. I discovered that if a cat can experience that many lives, then love can survive the best and worst of times. We all lose heart and there are times we can feel the need to give up, but true love carries us through the darkest moments so we can appreciate honor and truth in its most beautiful fashion.

The Enduring Love Through Nine Lives

In my first life I lived there was
So much chaos and frustration
Yet there was a spiritual love I always felt
Pulling me through long nights of desperation

In my second life I felt like I was
Drowning under a world of utter defeat
Yet a gentle, loving energy never left my side
And gave me the strength to get back on my feet

In my third life I walked around being a victim
Of constant lies and rejection
Yet I could feel a special energy take my hand
Leading me in a more positive direction

In my fourth life I felt as if nobody knew
How to really listen to my worries
Yet I felt an uplifting presence encouraging me
I was worthy enough to keep sharing my stories

In my fifth life I never felt like I ever fit in

MAGICAL LOVE MESSAGES BETWEEN KINDRED SPIRITS

Because I was just too shy to try
Yet despite my fears a caring spirit
Loved me enough so I could find peace despite asking why

In my sixth life I cried so much
I felt I was going to melt under all my tears
Yet a warm touch from a friendly soul
Was kind enough to comfort me through all my fears

In my seventh life I felt so weak that
I could barely face each passing day
Yet somehow I received a dream each night
From a serene spirit giving me hope that all would be ok

In my eighth life I was full of stress
And wondering how could I ever make it alone
Yet in my mind I could hear a sweet voice whisper
I will always keep you safe in your home

In my ninth life where I presently live
And often ask what my purpose may be
Through every season that has passed
I know there is a kindred spirit I love and trust so faithfully

Chapter 23 - The Healing Nature of a Soulmate's Touch

Magical Message #23: Sometimes all we need is that healing touch from someone we love and trust so much.

If there are two words that go together it would be the word soulmate and touch as they both have the power to bring healing to a soul in need of renewal. When a real soulmate truly cares about you, one simple touch can enlighten your soul. Sometimes we need to feel the warmth of a caring touch just to know someone cares and loves us.

In the following poem, "The Healing Nature of a Soulmate's Touch", the story is told of a lost soul in desperate need of feeling love and affection from someone he cherishes most. What he discovers is a kind of spiritual touch that comes through the beauty and power of nature. Through beautiful acts of nature, he soon realizes that he is not alone as the one he loves and cherishes most is always right there by his side through the best and worst of times.

This poem will help you realize that a spirit of love is always by your side.

The Healing Nature of a Soulmate's Touch

I was feeling so distraught
Not knowing what I should do
All I can remember was lying helpless on the sandy shore
Of a beach near home just needing you

As I lay calmly on the sand
That had become my temporary home
I looked right into the sky and could feel a cool breeze
Caress my soul so I did not feel all alone

With tears in my eyes I wondered when
God would let me feel your sweet touch
He whispered just look around and you will see
The one you love so much

In a brief moment I saw a nice seagull
Flying with grace above me
It was then I could feel your healing energy
Of peace calm my restless soul drowning in misery

Then I looked around me and saw
A few broken seashells that lay quietly in the sand
I could feel you whisper I know what it is like
To feel broken and as if nobody understands

I somehow could not stop crying because
I just wanted to heal from all the pain I had endured
Before I could tell what happened another seagull
Looked right at me with eyes so pure

I decided to close my eyes to see if maybe you
Would come see me in an imaginary escape
Then before I knew what to do I could hear you telling me
That we all make a lot of mistakes.

As I listened to the waves
Crashing softly on the beach
You embraced the depth of my soul with
An energy of love that no longer felt out of reach.

I looked deep within to see the ways
You had touched my weary heart
When I felt as if I could not go on your love
Reassured me you needed me right from the start

I felt as if I could not survive
One more moment of distress
Then the deeper I searched my soul
Your magical touch helped me endure life's tests.

MAGICAL LOVE MESSAGES BETWEEN KINDRED SPIRITS

In the midst of my pain and desire
To find something to make me whole
I looked deeper inside and felt your healing touch
In a way where your love would never let me go

What seemed to feel broken and shattered inside
Did not seem to keep me feeling so sad
Something about the way you touched my heart
Lifted me up and made me feel truly glad

When I opened my eyes it felt as if
The world was no longer so dark and weary
Somehow I was able to get back on my feet
Knowing that my life was no longer so dreary

I stretched my arms high into the air and took
The deepest breath my soul had ever been given
It was then I knew the love linking our souls
Had helped me know life really was worth living

Chapter 24 - The Home that Kept Us Together

_____

Magical Message #24: Home is always where the heart is as it serves as the place where we can release our burdens and connect with someone we love who knows us best.

The cliche that home is where the heart is is so true as it serves as the one place where we can embrace a safe haven away from all the chaos and stresses of life. Sometimes we all long for a place to which we can escape in hopes that we can protect ourselves from all the crazy issues that try to bring us down. Within our homes we all need to feel that there is someone there who truly loves and respects us for the ways we approach and enjoy this life.

In the following poem, "The Home that Kept Us Together", you will find a story of two women who were very close. They were sisters and yet they were the best of friends. No matter what life threw their way, they also managed to find time to spend with one another away from the pressures of a world filled with much chaos and hardship.

Through many different seasons of life, these two women discovered their family ties and deep friendship kept them rooted in a strong bond of joy and kindness where they could enjoy the very best treasures of life through the home of love and peace that keep their connection close and forever solid.

The Home that Kept us Together

Once upon a time there was a house
I once could call home
It was an elegant castle surrounded by cool, crystal water
So fresh nobody could leave it alone

I can close my eyes and be reminded
Of a place where you and I once played
Somehow your presence was the key
To keeping all my blues and problems away

We were children growing up
In a place so many wanted to be
You were my sister and good friend with whom
I trusted to share life's triumphs and tragedies

There were men and women of great grace

And stature trying to take what was ours
Yet you and I found solace walking and playing
In the midst of our home's decorative flowers

I remembered walking with you around the pond
Where sweet birds greeted us with love
They sensed the bond we shared was a connection
Keeping us together with ties from God above

Sometimes I wanted to cry so much
Because I felt nobody could understand
Yet you knew how to sit right beside me
And encourage me like nobody else can

In times when the whole world was against me
And I did not know what to do
You were the glue of hope holding me together
Through good times and sadness too

No matter where I turned and no matter
How hard my life could be
We could walk through the garden of flowers
That lined the path of our save haven so lovingly

There were secrets we both knew
That nobody else would ever get
You and I had a way of bearing our souls with
Such truth that we never had any regrets

In times of trials and times when it seemed

MAGICAL LOVE MESSAGES BETWEEN KINDRED SPIRITS

I had nobody on my side
You embraced me so gracefully that your warmth
Could put an end to all the challenging times

I remember so much about the special ways
You and I could have a picnic on warm, spring days
The rest of the world was chaotic, but we just
Held on to each other despite society's crazy ways

I am thankful for the special home
Where you and I could grow up together
We shared a beautiful connection that to this moment
Keeps our spirits linked forever

Chapter 25 - The Homeless Friend I Call Sunset

Magical Message #25: Sometimes the most precious comforts of this life come in the sweet, loving company of a pet we treasure so much.

I have learned in my life not to underestimate the true, loving connection that a pet can bring into our lives. Animals really do have this special way of making us feel loved when the rest of the world has left us broken and in despair. Sometimes all it takes is the warm touch of an animal to help us realize that we are not alone and that there is someone out there to watch over us when we need it most.

The following poem, "The Homeless Friend I Call Sunset", is based on a true story in my life as it is about a homeless, orange cat I found one day after my cat of 16 years, Jasper whom I wrote about previously, had passed away. I was driving home one evening in the late summer when I saw this cute, orange cat just laying at the edge of a parking lot. I was feeling quite empty after losing my cat of many years so when I saw this beautiful orange tabby, I was immediately drawn to him. From the moment I saw this cat, I decided to call him Sunset since that is the time of evening when I discovered him.

Ever since my discovery, Sunset became more than just a homeless cat to me, as he became my friend who always greeted with me such love and affection and was there for me when I just needed a true friend. Eventually, I lost Sunset as he was adopted to live in a better environment than the one he had suffered in for so long.

To this day I truly miss Sunset, but the following poem reflects what this special cat taught me along the way.

The Homeless Friend I Call Sunset

I was feeling completely down
And not sure of what to do
Then to my surprise I caught
A most precious glimpse of you

After the hole in my heart that was left
From one furry friend's death

Somehow I knew I needed something peaceful
To encourage me not to give up just yet

I was driving aimlessly around town
Trying to figure out the purpose of my life
In the middle of my confusion I wondered
If I would ever understand why

No matter how hard I tried to understand
The path where I was meant to go
Something about a yellow cat like you
Just completely embraced my grieving soul

I looked you in the eye and knew
That you really needed a friend
In my crazy life you helped me not lose hope
That my wounded heart would mend

I could tell you were hungry and so very wanting
Someone to acknowledge you were there
When the rest of the world ignored you
I wanted you to find a friend in me that truly did care

I was crying from the inside not really sure
Of the direction I should take
Yet somehow you walked a little closer to me
As if you sensed my heart was about to break

I could look you in the eye and felt a connection
To the friend I had lost and had loved so much

MAGICAL LOVE MESSAGES BETWEEN KINDRED SPIRITS

Though you were scared to let me pet you
I felt your reassuring energies like a warm, heartfelt touch

Day by day I felt led to come see you
Just to make sure you were ok
Seeing you lick your paws with grace made me
Feel that all my troubles would slowly melt away

Every evening I knew I could come to the place
Where you found refuge to give you food and drink
Just watching you sit and look at me with eyes of gratitude
Made it easier for me to relax and think

Now as each and every day begins
And the evening begins to fall
I found a special friend named Sunset
To help me finally make sense of it all

Chapter 26 - The Leaves of Love

_____

Magical Message #26: Don't ever discount the power of nature to heal your broken heart with love.

There are days when we all feel like just giving up. There are times it seems nobody truly understands how we feel. There are moments when all we really want is to just know someone somewhere truly cares for us. Throughout my lifetime, I have had many times where I felt so much great love and support, yet there have been so many times when I felt so misunderstood.

During one of my moments of feeling truly misunderstood, I was sitting alone in my car one day in the fall of the year with my windows open. To my surprise, two beautiful red leaves blew right in through the windows right before my eyes. As I watched these leaves lay peacefully side by side, I could feel an energy of

true relaxation come upon me as I realized that even
leaves find a way to stay connected when the winds of life
try to blow them apart.

Because I needed to feel a renewed sense of connection to
the universe, I decided to write the following poem, "The
Leaves of Love" as it helped me understand how nature
can whisper words of comfort in our souls when we need
it most.

The Leaves of Love

I was sitting in my car one afternoon
In the colorful, crisp fall
When the winds of change blew through my window
With an enticing, spiritual call

As the winds and the colorful leaves
Were blowing to and fro
Two bright, red leaves flew right into my window
With a magical and sparkling glow

I could feel the first leaf was sent my way
To let me know the spiritual world was real
Somewhere in the midst of my craziness
I needed a reminder what love was like to feel

This leaf peacefully glided right beside me
To help me stop and take a moment to really rest

Despite all my struggles I knew God was encouraging me
To hang in there to face another test

I watched in silence as this red leaf
Seemed to stay closely by my side
It was as if it knew how to comfort all my worries
To put all my anxiety out of my mind

Then to my surprise another pretty red leaf
Blew right in my window beside its friend
I could feel this leaf was trying to help me realize
What it was like to feel understood again

As the two lovely leaves lay side by side
With such charm and grace
I felt how much they loved each other in a world
Torn apart by chaos and deceptive ways

For a moment in time I pictured as if I was that leaf
That had fallen from the tree of solidarity
Somehow I knew I needed a new start in life
Where I could gain a much stronger clarity

The longer I stared at these two lovely leaves
The more I knew God sent them to give me peace
He could feel I had been trapped too long in a world
Full of pain and constant misery

I picked up the leaves and watched how
Their glorious aura sparkled before my eyes

No matter how much the storms of life had tried
To break them they had a faith that would never die

I drove away that day with my new friends
Leaving a spirit of change lingering in my soul
Now had come the time to release the past
And embrace a new path for me to go

Chapter 27 – The Life Raft and the Yellow Bird that Saved My Soul

_____

Magical Message #27: Sometimes we all need something safe to hold on to in order to help get us through the tough times.

In everyday life it seems the struggles we encounter are endless. One day it can seem we are on top of the world and the next it seems we have hit rock bottom. No matter where we fall on this spectrum, it is important that we learn how to understand the true beauty that exists between God and the signs He often sends to show His great love for us, enough love to save us from the world and even from the dark abyss that exists within us.

The following poem, "The Life Raft and the Yellow Bird that Saved My Soul", is a narrative poem about a struggling soul who is literally floating upon a life raft desperately looking for someone somewhere to help him

feel safe. When it seems all hope is lost, God sends a
yellow bird to help his friend in distress.

If anything, this poem helps us realize that when we feel
on the verge of giving up, a moment of true rescue
eventually comes.

The Life Raft and The Yellow Bird that Saved My Soul

I was floating down the river of life
Wishing the current of water would not be so rough
I kept thinking back to my past when it felt
I really had experienced more than enough

I was holding onto my life raft as if
It was the only thing I had to really trust
No matter where the current took me
I knew at some point I needed some much better luck

I kept bumping into rocks every where I turned
On the raging river of my despair
Somehow I just wished I could convince myself
That life is not always so fair

I tried to dodge the broken tree limbs of pain
That seemed intent on knocking me down
As sad I as I was feeling I wanted so much
To get rid of my continual frown

The river of life just kept raging more and more

HEATHER D. WRIGHT

As the winds of great distress blew my way
For some reason I knew I had no control
Over my fate no matter what I did to feel ok

The sky grew cloudy above me and great storms
Threatened the journey I felt too weak to take
In so many ways I just felt how could God
Save my hurting soul when I've made so many mistakes

I kept holding onto this life raft praying
God would lead me safely home
Before I knew what happened I saw a small yellow bird
Flying right above me so I did not feel so alone

The river kept raging and the storms of life
Seemed so scary I felt like having a fit
Yet each time I thought I should give up
My life raft and the yellow bird would not let me quit

There were moments of great distress
I honestly felt I was just going to die
My life raft collected my weary tears and the yellow bird
Never left me when all I could do was cry

After a long, hard journey where I
Never thought I would make it through
When I held on to my life raft and trusted my sweet friend
I realized sometimes life is good to you

Somewhere in the midst of all

MAGICAL LOVE MESSAGES BETWEEN KINDRED SPIRITS

My stress and constant worry
I kept the faith I would make it safely to the river bank
Of serenity if I did not get in such a hurry

When I finally made it to the safe shores
Of the river bank that brought my spirit peace of mind
I thanked God for giving me a good raft to hold onto
And a true friend who never left my side

Chapter 28 - The Little Yellow Bird With the Key to My Heart

Magical Message #28: Sometimes God sends us the comfort of love in the presence of one of nature's finest creatures.

In life we often experience times when it seems nobody understands us. There are moments when it can seem we are lost even among the largest crowd of people. I believe that God created nature as a comfort to us when it feels that we need a special friend to let us know we are truly loved and respected in our darkest times of need.

In the following poem, "The Little Yellow Bird With the Key to My Heart", you will find the sweet story of a yellow bird who befriends a sad soul who has become broken due to many of life's greatest hardships.

In need of more love in his life, this special bird becomes

his trusted companion and friend who stands by his side letting him know that he is always there for him. In fact, this bird is the spirit of a lost love that comes back to surround his former lover with eternal love and protection.

You never know when a force of nature is in essence the spirit of a loved one whose heart once beat in tune with your own.

The Little Yellow Bird With the Key to My Heart

There was a little yellow bird that
Always seems to know when I need a friend
It comes to my little feeder everyday when
My life feels sad and lost all over again

In times of pain and my
Greatest moments of distress
This little yellow bird sits on my feeder
As if to give me serene moments of peace and true rest

He is more than a friend but someone
I had loved many lives ago
The love I feel when I see him warms
The heart of my broken spirit in need of love to grow

This little yellow bird always comes
To my feeder when I need to feel something real

It is amazing how he knows I need to feel the touch
Of a magical love to keep my restless heart still

This little yellow bird never seems
To want to leave my side
It is like it knows exactly when to fly to my feeder
When I need to feel strong and emotionally alive

I can just watch it for hours wondering
What message it has to bring
Somehow this little bird completes the other part
Of my soul left alone without a happy song to sing

Sometimes I watch this little yellow bird
As it feeds its little body with the right food
Even when I don't feel that great
It uplifts my spirits to put me in a better mood

I am not sure from where this
Little yellow bird has come or why
All I know is it carries an essence of peace
I cannot find among others who have left me to cry

For all my life I have been on a search
To find a love that is true
When I look at this little yellow bird on my feeder
I can feel the love you hold for me I also carry for you

No matter how long the days and nights
Are that seem to pass me by

When I need to feel the depth of true love
This little yellow bird comes to me at just the right time

Chapter 29 - The Love Story Between a Seagull and a Broken Soul

---

Magical Message #29: Sometimes all it takes is the right touch at the right time by the right soul to help us heal from a broken heart.

We have all been there when someone we really thought loved us just broke our heart into a million pieces. We have all experienced the agony of thinking we found the person who we feel will comfort us only to leave us feeling alone drowning in our own misery.

Then comes along someone or something different to give us hope again. Sometimes the right person or situation develops just when we need a good sign to keep us going when we often feel like giving up.

The following poem "A Love Story Between a Seagull

and a Broken Soul" is a beautiful story about someone
whose heart has been shattered by empty promises
longing for someone or something to make her heart feel
whole again. Then she meets a special seagull who she
feels is sent by God to help her heal from her pain
knowing her life is important and that she is truly loved.

The Love Story Between a Seagull and a Broken Soul

I was sailing on the ocean
Away from all of my worries
Yet something inside me said don't give up
Because you are headed for a new set of stories

Frustrated and feeling as if
My life was just one big lie
I felt maybe it would be best if
I just gave up and had one continuous cry

I was crying so much
From the inside out
I could feel all the anger within me
Take control that all I could do was scream out

In my sailboat of hope
Away from my totally crazy life
I just kept hoping I could find a way
Through my struggles without having to always ask why

As I sailed on the ocean of new dreams

Knowing at some point things would have to change
Somehow within my weary spirit
I knew something had to give before I went insane

I prayed so loud and asked God to send me
Some kind of sign everything would be ok
All of a sudden a beautiful seagull flew down
Into my sailboat that I so wanted to save

He just looked me right in the eyes
With tears as if he truly knew my pain
I fell in love with him right away
Because I felt he could protect my good name

I asked him why I always seemed to feel
Like I was so alone on an island of false dreams
He flapped his wings knowing how hard it is
To be happy when life is coming apart at the seams

Upset and worried that my life would
Never be the kind of peace I so need to embrace
The precious seagull that became my friend
Gently touched my arm with such love I was blown away

Somehow even though I was completely wounded
From those I really thought did care
I held the seagull in my arms with such passion
Because I needed a true love to really be there

He and I had a way of communicating

MAGICAL LOVE MESSAGES BETWEEN KINDRED SPIRITS

That the rest of the world could never possess
As tired as I was of a broken heart this seagull knew
How to reassure me there was no need to stress.

I knew at some point I would have to face
A new life and leave my present world behind
The seagull just flew right above my sailboat
Leading me with great love to a much better life

I finally made it across the great sea of healing waters
With a new love that cared so much
He and I grew to love one another so greatly
We could connect without words with a simple touch

I began to walk on the new shores of renewed hope
Knowing I would never be all alone
God sent me the precious gift of real love
In my true friend the seagull I could call my own

Everywhere I go and everywhere I turn my special love
Is always flying close to my side
Even if the walls of despair begin to cave in
I know the seagull and I will love each other until we die

Chapter 30 - The Lover of My Soul

Magical Message #30: We must realize that God has a way of sending us signs through nature that we are truly admired and loved.

God has a way of loving our souls through the best and worst of times. Sometimes we must pay attention to nature as I feel it often speaks to our souls when we truly need to feel the power of a love that never leaves or forsakes us.

The following poem, "The Lover of My Soul" is all about a journey of one person trying to feel a connection to someone or something that can help him get through his own moments of despair and solitude. He finds that nobody truly understands him, and he is desperate to feel something within nature to help him feel at peace.

There are times in life that we often fail to realize just how loved we truly are. It is important for each of use to take note of the special ways we are loved when we often do not even realize it, yet the joy it can bring us is beyond measure.

The Lover of My Soul

There was a force in the universe
Pulling me through channels of time
As I lifted my hands into the air I felt
A karmic connection touched my heart with nice signs

I closed my eyes and felt the cool, gentle breeze
Of a wind that came from a place I felt I had known
Somewhere in the midst of the storms around me
I felt a voice calling me to come back home

I opened my eyes and decided to walk a path
That so few could understand
It seemed a lonely path to go for me
But yet I could feel the touch of a warm, friendly hand

Upon my path through woods with trees
Whose leaves had fallen to the ground
My eyes were drawn to their colors of peace
To calm my inner cries that had the most frustrating sound

I walked a little further and saw a yellow butterfly
Who seemed to have traveled far to find me

It was if it had a special key to my soul
To lessen the power of my innermost misery

With a smile on my face somehow I felt
There was more to this life than all the pain I had faced
I kept walking this path of self-discovery
When a red bird caught my eye on a limb with such grace

This red bird just flapped its wings a time or two
As if to tell me it knew I had been hurt in the past
I just watched him intently with eyes of gratitude
Because it cared about me in a way that would last

With such contentment I felt maybe this path
I felt led to travel was meant for me to keep walking
The path upon which I walked seemed free
From empty promises and hopeless talking

As I walked further into the woods on this path
That now became my new story
I looked up and saw the sun breaking through
The clouds to free my spirit from all my worry

When I walked right into the light I closed my eyes
And let the rays of the sun warm my weary soul
In the midst of my struggles I felt something
Pulling on my heart with a love that would not let me go

It was like all the forces of nature I had met
Were pulling me closer to the love that had never died

MAGICAL LOVE MESSAGES BETWEEN KINDRED SPIRITS

Even though I could not see the lover of my soul
I felt you reaching for me through passages of time

I spent so much of my life trying to find a love
That is stronger than anything I had ever embraced
On this new path you were the spiritual force
In the creations of nature who never let me feel disgraced

A spiritual love exists between our souls that
Surpasses every battle and unfortunate setback
In the midst of my travels, I found the lover of my soul
That had the right heart to get me back on track

I often wonder why it took me so long
To find a connection that fits my heart so well
The lover of my soul and I have a karmic love story
That will never fail

Chapter 31 - The Loving Link Between Kindred Souls

Magical Message #31: Love is often felt through a connection that may not exist in the physical realm, but its strength is felt powerfully through spiritual means.

In a world so focused on physical gratification, it is no wonder people think that love is all about what can satisfy us in physical ways. We think someone who loves us has to prove his or her love by showering us with lots of physical items. It is almost as if we think we need to have something in our possession in order to feel better about ourselves.

Sometimes people think materialistic pleasures can satisfy them when in all actuality they just make us all feel empty inside. There are times we just need to feel something deeper and something so powerful that comes from a force outside of ourselves. The greatest source of love is the one that exists within the realm of the spiritual world. In this world, the most powerful connections exist between like-minded souls.

In the following poem, "The Loving Link Between Kindred Souls", it speaks of a connection between two special spirits whose deep love helps them embrace their true destiny to feel loved and protected at all times.

The Loving Link Between Kindred Souls

From the time God breathed
New life into my soul
I never knew how my hard journey in life
Could cause my heart to grow so cold

Everyday I wondered how was I going
To make it through
Somehow God knew I needed a change
In my life to find a love that was honestly true

I lived so many lifetimes where I could feel
A special presence by my side
Through every path I walked your love
Gave me the strength to overcome my pride

Everyday I felt like I was walking along a path
That was too hard for me to see

I had tears in my eyes begging God
To free me from all my misery

In so many ways I struggled to find
Something to make me feel complete
Yet everyone I thought I could trust
Betrayed me deeply and left me lost in a world of defeat

Sometimes I have prayed for a chance to escape
The life that has become my prison
All I ever needed was a change of pace
And a much more hopeful vision

I cannot recall all the lifetimes
God allowed me to live without regret
But I could always feel a spirit of love around me
That was too intense for me to forget

In each life I lived I can remember feeling
A magical warmth embrace the depth of my heart
No matter how hard life became there was a loving energy
Giving me hope right from the start

As I walk the road of this present life
God has given me to face
The desire I have to be close to your love
Is often my only saving grace

I can be on opposite sides of the world
And feel the connection that keeps us alive

MAGICAL LOVE MESSAGES BETWEEN KINDRED SPIRITS

Just feeling you reach for my hand when I feel lost
Is the direction I need almost every time.

In times when I feel that nobody
Really knows me at all
I can feel you whisper how much you will
Always be there to protect me from a tragic fall

It seems the closer I try to connect
With the love I know that keeps us in sync
There is always a jealous energy vampire
Trying to pull me away with a deceptive instinct

In the real world we live there will always
Be people expecting us to play a part
Yet your love is the charming remedy I need
When I am lost in the dark

I could search the world over and never find
A love that keeps me so strong and feeling at ease
The love we share between our souls is
God's beautiful creation keeping us together in peace

Chapter 32 - The Magical Love Destiny Between Twin Souls

———————

Magical Message #32: Every true love in life is part of a powerful destiny.

I truly feel love and destiny flow together in perfect harmony. After all, if love is right then destiny will feel right as well. We have all experienced different types of relationships with many different kinds of people, and yet love is the one that seems to mystify so many. Some people think they must latch on to whomever they can find just so they can fit into society's mold of what it thinks a relationship should be.

The following poem, "The Magical Love Destiny Between Twin Souls", is all about the difference between what the world's perception of love is versus the beautiful and unconditional love felt between two souls destined to

———

love each other from now until eternity. It is a narrative poem depicting the contrast between false love versus true love and how a real, heartfelt love can help us embrace the destined relationship path upon which we are meant to travel.

The Magical Love Destiny Between Twin Souls

There is a love that surpasses
All kinds of connections
It has a spiritual magic that enhances the air
With much magnetic attraction

Some people search their whole lives over
To find something real and true
Because we all get tired of liars and fake souls
Who make you feel used

There is a love that God created
From the very beginning of time
It has its own rhythm and keeps those
Destined hearts together with an honest rhyme

Some people think they find love
In the most traditional of places
Yet true connection is a spiritual dance
Keeping the right hearts together in good graces

There is a love that never seems to die
Because it echoes to a tune that nobody else understands

HEATHER D. WRIGHT

When two like-minded souls connect
They feel the warmth of real, caring hands

In times of trials and much hopeless searching
When life seems much confusing
The love between twin souls is the treasure to surpass
All pain and false illusions

There is a love that can satisfy your soul so deeply
That nobody could ever really fulfill
When the right connection is made
Twin lovers will know that their love is always so real

Many people never get the chance to experience
A love that can change their lives forever
Even if they can't live in this world their spiritual dance
Is the tie that always holds them together

There is a love that has its own language
That can be shared without many words
When one feels sad his twin soul can calm his fears
With the most comforting songs ever heard

In a time where everyone thinks that finding the one
Is based on tradition and what all thinks is best
The twin souls can love deeply through a mystic dream
To put each others' worries to rest

There is a love that seems to surpass all the
Ups and downs in this crazy life we all endure

MAGICAL LOVE MESSAGES BETWEEN KINDRED SPIRITS

There is a mutual understanding without words
Where twin souls keep each other feeling reassured

From one lifetime to the next so few often
Find the other half to their hungry souls
But in the world between twin souls there is no time lost
And an energy of never letting each other go

There is a love that so many desire
And yet so few ever get to enjoy
Yet the twin soul's love is an enthusiastic dance
Among equals that is as precious as a child's new toy

There is a love without limits
That contains an unbreakable emotional energy
In a world where true love is doubted
Twin souls remain connected by a magical love destiny

Chapter 33 - The Music Box Connection

Magical Message #33: Sometimes we need to escape into a fantasy world to feel the touch of a love that nobody or nothing can take from us.

I have always been a romantic at heart fascinated by the many tales of romance that caught my eye on many different TV shows and movies I have watched over time. Even though life does not always have a fairy tale ending, sometimes I think it is ok to create one in our hearts and minds. I am not only a romantic at heart, but I am also a dreamer and can escape into a fairy tale world very quickly.

Because of my imaginative and romantic approach to life, I decided one day to write the following poem, "The Music Box Connection" which is all about one person's escape into a music box that turns into a great love story. Within this music box, the wandering soul discovers the presence of a loving spirit with whom he falls in love and with whom he shares the beautiful music of peace and harmony. What starts as a journey into a simple music box becomes a whole new way of life filled with the most powerful love connecting two hearts meant to love each other for eternity.

The Music Box Connection

In the middle of the night
I could hear such a sweet sound
Interested to find out what I was hearing
I got out of bed and looked around

I looked high and low for the source
Of this harmonious melody
What I finally discovered was a beautiful music box
That sparked my curiosity

As I opened the music box I was suddenly
Taken inside to a brand new place
I felt I was not alone and the one
I had always loved was not far away

Inside this box I saw a bright golden path
Enticing me to keep walking without fear
The music played serenely as a voice cried
I am your kindred spirit who has always been here

I came across a symphony playing the most
Joyous sounds I had ever known
Then I could feel a sweet voice whisper
You will feel my undying love and know you are not alone

As the music played a melody
I truly did not want to end
I could feel you reach down to grab my hand
Like a most trusted friend

As I walked around the music box
I came across a ballet where grace and beauty met
Then I felt a soft embrace around my soul say
Do not give up because the best is to come yet

I strolled then to a park where so many musicians
Were playing instruments without reservation
You reached inside my soul and said
I will love your forever without any hesitation

I walked right through a concert
Where the music was loud and full of life
Yet I did not feel scared because in the chaos
You whispered I will protect you at night

Before I knew what to do I ended up on a stage
Where the whole world expected me to sing
I could feel you calm my beating heart with a reassurance
I was good enough to endure anything

MAGICAL LOVE MESSAGES BETWEEN KINDRED SPIRITS

As the music box continued to play a lullaby
That soothed my searching soul
I ended up in a field of daisies with you
Right by my side promising never to let me go

When I closed my eyes I prayed
This musical venture would last forever
I decided to live within the music box
Where we were free to love each other like a treasure

I could hear the rest of the world looking for you
And me on the outside of our new home
Despite their constant cries to force us back
Into the present world we were determined not to go

I smiled at you and you smiled at me
With the kind of loyalty and trust so many never find
The music box that led us down this new journey
Remains the link keeping our love alive

Chapter 34 - The Mysterious Cat and Two Connected Spirits

Magical Message #34: We should never underestimate the power of an animal to remind us that true love never dies.

As a cat lover, I have learned that cats are truly some of God's most precious animals as they have a special way of bringing true friendship into our lives. I also feel so many of the cats I owned growing up had a magical way of blessing my life because there were many times I felt I had known certain cats I was around from another time and place.

In the same fashion, just as cats could be connected to us from another lifetime, I also feel we have each shared special lives with others who often cross our paths again. The following poem, "The Mysterious Cat and Two Connected Spirits", is a story about one special cat whose

owner sparks memories of another life where he shared
this same cat with someone he loved very much.

This narrative poem is a story of connecting the present
with the past knowing that one special animal was
destined to remind its owner that true love never dies.

The Mysterious Cat and Two Connected Spirits

Once upon a time there was a special cat
Who was looking for a home
It was as if she had lived with me in another time and place
For which I longed to remember so

I felt drawn to this orange cat
Unlike any pet I had ever had
This one was so calm and relaxed as if she knew
How to make me feel safe and truly glad

Years have passed and this cat
Has never left my side
In times I have been sad she carries a warm place
Inside her heart that never dies

Sometimes I feel that life is always a roller coaster
Full of emotional ups and downs
Yet my special cat can sense when
I need a friend to just be sure to hang around

As the times with my loving cat have passed

I could sense something was different about her eyes
When she looked at me it was as if she carried
The secret to a previous kind of life

In my cat's eyes I saw a reflection of another
Creative soul to whom I felt especially drawn
My memories took me back where the spirit, cat, and I
Lived under a different set of laws

I can remember finding this cat
And how it stumbled upon my path
Then I carried it to my kindred spirit
Who was my companion never letting me lose track

For some reason I felt this cat was meant
For my kindred soul and I to keep
During each moment she was the kind presence
Giving us the strength to truly be at peace

In the light of day I had flashbacks to how
This cat followed my kindred soul everywhere she walked
I still hear faint whispers of my kindred spirit
Sharing her dreams while the cat listened as she talked

When the days were beautiful and the sun
Brightened the sky with its lovely ways
I remembered the picnics we all had together
While the cat just danced around us and played

In the evenings when the sun would set

MAGICAL LOVE MESSAGES BETWEEN KINDRED SPIRITS

And the night would come to pass
I remembered the cat sat right between my soulmate
And I with a peaceful link that would last

It was if we lived in our own world
That nobody could tear apart
My kindred spirit and I could both hold our cat
Knowing she would protect our connected hearts

Memories kept flooding my mind of the days
The cat walked with my kindred spirit and I everywhere
Even when my kindred soul and I were upset
We survived our problems because our cat truly cared

Now that I live in a different time and place
I know my kindred spirit and I were truly happy together
My friend the cat remains the link to my kindred soul
Uniting us in a love destined to last forever

Chapter 35 - The Night a Soulmate Rescued My Heart

Magical Message #35: Sometimes we must reach into the depth of our hearts and souls to embrace the love we were always meant to have.

I have found that so many people prefer to let their heads rule their hearts rather than the other way around. It seems so many people are afraid to let the power of great love inside for fear of getting hurt. We live in a world that is drowning in negative energy, and yet, there is a beautiful spiritual energy that exists which can turn our despair into great hope.

In the following poem, "The Night a Soulmate Rescued My Heart", you will find the story of an unhappy soul seeking for greater love in her life. She feels as if everyone and everything has let her down and hopes to find true love in the midst of her sadness. When she decides to let go of her mind telling her love always leads to pain, she then reaches within the depths of her heart and discovers a special connection of love that never leaves her and brings her joy when she needs it most.

As I have discovered, it's ok sometimes to wish for a divine rescue of love when it seems all hope is lost.

The Night a Soulmate Rescued My Heart

In the midst of a cool night
In the middle of the fall
I placed my hand over my heart
Hoping you would hear me call

In the blink of an eye I could
Feel you reach for my hand
It was as if your magical touch was the life force
Giving me strength to keep going again

As I lay my head
Down to sleep
I could feel you wrap your arms around me
To make sure my soul was at peace

In the escape
Of a special dream
You entered into my astral world
Making sure there was someone to take care of me

In the journey of a dream
Into another world and time
You held my hand so nothing could break
The bond keeping us in sync to a harmonious rhyme

Within my dream I knew that there
Was nothing that could keep us apart
I could feel the way you loved me was the
Unconditional flame that would protect my heart

After my dream
Came to an end
I found tears in my eyes hoping you
Would just come by my side once again

As I got up to face another long hard day
Not sure how I would make it through
I could feel your loving energy surrounding me
With words of hope that you would always be true

I felt lost in a crowd of people all trying
To pull me in so many crazy directions
Then I could feel your strong energy reassure me
That you would always be my greatest protection

At the end of a tough day when I felt that
My fears and worries were too great to bear
I could hear you whisper words of comfort
That you would always be there

MAGICAL LOVE MESSAGES BETWEEN KINDRED SPIRITS

As the sun began to set and give way
To another quiet night
I could feel your powerful love breathing into my soul
That everything would be all right

When I lay my head down to try
And find some much needed rest
I felt you reach for my hand just to say
Together our souls would pass life's greatest tests

Chapter 36 - The Painting on the Wall

Magical Message #36: Often we are given signs that hold the answers to a previous lifetime where kind souls we once loved still surround us today with great emotional support.

I believe God gives us signs of many things in this life. I feel we have all lived many lives before this one, and that in at least one of those lives we have crossed paths with someone very special whose very presence gives up hope in the midst of darkness.

The following poem, "The Painting on the Wall Between Loving Souls", tells a story about a young man who is traveling for work only to notice a unique painting hanging on a wall in his hotel room. The longer he observes this painting, the more he feels the picture before him reminds him of a familiar place and time. Through his imagination he finds himself drawn into the

world of this painting where he crosses paths with
someone to whom he feels a powerful, loving bond.

As his past life and present world collide, this man
discovers a love from a another lifetime that he finds
provides a place of refuge in his present world. He comes
to realize that the love he found in a past lifetime still
keeps him feeling happy and safe in this one.

The Painting on the Wall Between Loving Souls

There is a painting on a wall
From another place and time
It seems to have the echo of a past where
I once lived to a much more peaceful rhyme

I remember walking around a pond
Where life seemed truly at peace
When life seemed too much I just sat beside the water
To put my restless mind at ease

There were trees in my midst that seemed to speak
Another language that made me glad
Somehow in the midst of my frustration
They could release the feelings making me so sad

In a minute I could close my eyes and feel
The air just carry me through the lands before me
It seemed to whisper we will keep you grounded
And free you from all your misery

Everywhere I went in this land
Of new hopes and dreams
I finally realized that life is not always
The monotonous play that it often seems

As I lay in the grass hoping
To figure out the path of my life
I caught an image of you
Laying right by my side

In a moment where it seemed the whole world
Was frozen and everything did not seem ok
I felt you reach for my hand letting me know
There would come better days

I decided to take a walk down a path
Through this land where life seemed a little fresher
With you walking right beside me
I knew I could handle all of life's pressures

As the sun kept shining on this path
Where you and I were meant to walk
It was if we could speak a special kind of language
Without words and superficial talk

I knew that somehow as I looked into this painting
On the wall you were right there
Despite all the careless chatter around me
You were the one who would always care

MAGICAL LOVE MESSAGES BETWEEN KINDRED SPIRITS

As my eyes were drawn to this painting
That portrayed a world where we were once together
I can still feel the connection we shared
Pulling me closer back to the love we would share forever

I don't always understand why things happen
Or why certain images catch my eye
Yet within my soul I feel the connection we share
Is stronger than all the unanswered whys

You hold the key to my heart that can unlock
Any mystery that tries to hurt my soul
When I look at the painting on the wall
I feel you by my side giving me strength to never let go

I am often reminded of the painting on the wall
That still makes me smile
The special memories of the land we shared
Gives me hope that our loving link will never die

Chapter 37 - The Past Life Love Connection

————————

Magical Message #37: We often experience the presence of love in many special ways because of connections to lifetimes we have endured before our present existence.

I love the power of a good dream as I feel it is a mystical way of escaping into another place and time where we can truly find peace. Dreams have always been known to be a reflection of our subconscious desires, and yet I feel they provide a journey into our hearts and souls to connect with something far greater and stronger than anything we could ever imagine.

In the following poem, "The Past Life Love Connection", you will find a story of someone whose dream takes her back through many different life experiences. Through these experiences, she finds herself crossing paths with a

true soulmate partner who helps her endure the best and
worst of times. Through this great shared love, both souls
are able to heal each other and give one another strength
no matter what comes their way.

For anyone truly wanting to know what true love really
feels like, this narrative poem holds the key to the kind of
love that never dies.

The Past Life Love Connection

I fell into a deep dream that took me
Far from the present place and time
Somehow I needed something more
To fill my restless soul with a more peaceful rhyme

I was not sure where my mystical journey
Was quite taking me
Yet I let the force of nature help me
Connect with you so relentlessly

Somehow in my heart I knew you and I
Had been together in a way others can't understand
Through my travels back in time I could feel
Your warm caring spirit always touching my hand

It seemed the decades and centuries were going
So fast I could not make out the lives I had lived
Yet in my past life travels I felt your presence
Encouraging me to be strong and always forgive

In one life I could feel that I felt
Too weak to ever go on
Yet I could hear you whisper the words
Of a sweet, loving melodious song

At another place and time I felt
The whole world was trying to bring me down
Yet I could sense your wise words helping me
Be strong and not let others run me out of town

In one special place I could see us sitting
Side by side in front of an ocean so calm and serene
It was as if all my inner fears were melted away
By your love that kept me falling apart so tragically

In another scene I was the life of the party
And the one always wanting to do things my way
Yet you were the voice of reason telling me
To be careful who I trusted so I did not feel ashamed

In another vision I could see us walking
Through a field of flowers where nobody could interrupt
In the midst of our isolation I could feel your love
Telling me to keep the faith and never give up

The next stop in my travels was one where
I seemed I was on top of the world with much strength
When others did not understand what I needed
You could speak to my soul on the same wavelength

MAGICAL LOVE MESSAGES BETWEEN KINDRED SPIRITS

In another life there were great wars
And people trying to tear other worlds apart
Yet in the middle of all those battles
I could feel your love embracing my heart

When I came to another stop on my travels
I was on an island surrounded by animals ready to kill
But no matter where I turned your love helped
Me find refuge and a safe place to heal

In one life I was surrounded by so many people
Who thought they knew me best
Yet no matter how much they drained my energies
Your sweet love helped me truly rest

I traveled back in time and found myself
In a circus where the whole world just kept spinning
As sick as I was your unconditional love
Kept me feeling lucky like my heart was always winning

Through every stop in my magical travels
Through past lives where you and I had been together
I woke up from this dream feeling confident
That the bond of love we shared would last forever

Through the ups and downs of my present life
When I really would love to just escape
I close my eyes and hold my hand over my heart
Feeling your love that I know will never go away

Chapter 38 - The Poetic Song Between Kindred Spirits

Magical Message #38: When two like-mind souls connect, they share a special poetic language that gives them the ability to encourage each other even when it feels the odds are against them.

I feel there are many ways in which we can express ourselves. As I have gotten older, I have come to appreciate the creative ways we can learn to communicate with those to whom we feel a special bond. Because kindred spirits share a special bond, I feel there is a poetic kind of language that only they can understand.

Poetry is the music of the soul to me, and I know that when you find a kindred spirit the language of the heart will never die. Kindred spirits remain connected for life,

and they always find a way to keep the flame of good
energies burning between them.

The following poem, "The Poetic Song Between Kindred
Spirits", is all about the special connection shared
between kindred spirits looking to rise above the
pressures of their daily lives to keep the beauty of their
bond alive in the midst of chaos and confusion.

The Poetic Song Between Kindred Spirits

I was feeling lost as can be
And wanted to find my way
Which led me to you on
My most desperate day

There have been highs and lows
But we always survive
We look for all things which
Will never divide

Others don't understand
The connection we share
And we will rise above and show them
We don't care

I am glad to know that you get me
In ways only we can understand
With you I can conquer the depths of despair
With you holding my hand

Together we are always feeling
So strong and free
Yes we can overcome any difficult circumstances
Without others, just you and me

What we have is
So precious and rare
We are there for one another now
Even when life is not fair

I will love you forever even when
The whole world is hard to endure
Our love is true and
Because of this we are sure

I want to make you happy and give you back
What you do for me some how some way
Keep the faith I will lead you on the right path
Trusting in the love you feel each day

Chapter 39 - The Rainbow Bridge to a Truly Missed Friend

_____

Magical Message #39: Sometimes losing a dear pet we love so much can feel like we are losing a part of ourselves until we discover that the connections to our furry friends never die.

Death is never easy to face as it is hard to let go of someone or something we love so much. Like so many of us, losing a beloved pet can be almost or just as hard as losing a family member or friend. Animals I feel are God's special creatures, and I feel they have the ability to touch our lives in the most magical of ways. However, when we lose a pet, it can feel as if a piece of our heart has been ripped out of our chest.

I have had many cats and dogs throughout my lifetime. However, there was one cat I had for 16 years, Jasper, that I wrote about previously. She and I became the best of friends from the time I got her as kitten, and she remained by my side throughout most of my adult life. Unfortunately, like everything that lives, it eventually must die. When Jasper got sick, I was able to spend the final hours of her life with her. When she took her last breath, I realized she was going to another world on the other side. Just as people go to Heaven when they die, I feel animals go to a special place that I discovered is called the Rainbow Bridge.

The following poem, "The Rainbow Bridge to a Truly Missed Friend", is all about the spirit world our beloved pets call home when their life in this world comes to an end, and as I have discovered with Jasper which is reflected in this poem, those pets we love and to which we feel a bond, remain in our hearts and souls forever.

The Rainbow Bridge to a Truly Missed Friend

I was looking for a way to escape all the
Suffering that tried to hold me down
Somehow I felt the friend I had loved
And lost was on the other side far from this town

There were so many detours along the way
That I was too unsure of where to go
Yet within my weary spirit I knew at some point
I would find a way to get back part of my lost soul

MAGICAL LOVE MESSAGES BETWEEN KINDRED SPIRITS

I came to a bridge that was in
A much different kind of place
Beyond the horizon was a bright rainbow behind
The bridge that seemed to bring a smile to my face

I had never seen a bridge quite so peaceful
And free from such pain
As I began to walk across, it felt like a gentler spirit
Was keeping me safe from unwanted shame

When I got to the middle of the bridge
I saw so many animals trying to catch my eye
There were birds, cats, dogs, and so many other creatures
Who caught me by pleasant surprise

I had a feeling that this was a new kind
Of Heaven where a different life existed
I knew no matter how much I was pulled back
To my current life that my soul completely resisted

I stood in the middle of the bridge taking
A deep breath as if this air could truly heal my soul
Deep within the very heart of my sad spirit
I knew God wanted me to keep the faith and not let go

I had all kinds of animals walking up to me
As if they wanted me to know it would be ok
My tears fell to the ground as if they knew I needed
To find some renewed strength along the way

HEATHER D. WRIGHT

So many animals seemed to just
Stay right by my side
I asked them if they happened to see my cat, Jasper
That not too long ago had died

With great pleasure they led me across the bridge
To a land full of flowers and a nearby stream
All the birds flying around me whispered to keep the faith
As Jasper would return to me

I walked around the nature trail around the water
But could not seem to find my once beloved cat
Before I knew what to do I saw her lying on a rock
Taking in the sun that warmed her furry back

I called out to my sweet Jasper
And her ears perked right up
She just meowed loudly and ran swiftly to greet me
As if fate meant for us both to have better luck

I picked her up into my arms and hugged her
As if we had never been apart
It was like all the sadness I felt went away
Because we were always connected from the start

When my alarm went off the next morning
I so wished this dream did not have to end
Because no matter what happened in this life
I would always miss my soul connected friend

Chapter 40 - The Red-winged Black Bird With a Special Kind of Love

---

Magical Message #40 – Sometimes a simple creature of nature can remind us of the beauty of love knowing there is a higher power looking out for us.

For most of my life, I have always been fascinated with birds as I feel they are God's special messengers meant to help us when we need it most. In my mind birds always represent a sense of freedom as they know how to fly above all the discouraging acts of nature that try to bring them down.

The following poem, "The Red-winged Black Bird With a Special Kind of Love", is actually inspired by real events in my own life. Not too far from where I live, there is a local park with a pond around which I have always enjoyed walking. On many occasions while walking around this pond, I was often greeted by a sweet red-winged black bird that seemed to fly in my midst during my frequent walks. Often it would sit calmly perched on a nearby tree, and every time I saw this bird I felt a sense of peace as I was usually feeling down and stressed about my own disappointments in this life. It seemed that every time I encountered this bird during my walks, I also felt a sense of compassion as I really thought that it was God's way of saying you are going to be ok as you have special spiritual forces looking out for you.

To this day, I have always been grateful for the red-winged black bird as it helped me to feel true serenity and great love during my most stressful moments. Because of this gratitude, I not only wrote the following poem, but I felt led to share this story of good energy with you.

The Red-winged Black Bird With A Special Kind of Love

There was a red-winged black bird
Perched on a tree close to me
He seemed to just watch me walk
As if he had a story to share so magically

As I walked around the pond
That had become my safe haven
This little bird whispered I know
What it feels like to be mistaken

MAGICAL LOVE MESSAGES BETWEEN KINDRED SPIRITS

Unsure of why this nice bird seemed
To follow me to every tree in my path
Every time our eyes connected I felt he was
Trying to tell me to stay strong and never look back

Sometimes I felt maybe this admirable
Bird was sent from God above
To help me keep the faith that there really
Exists a most unique kind of love

I walked a little further with
A few tears in my eyes
Then I caught a glimpse of my new found friend
Flapping his wings as if he could feel I wanted to cry

I thought to myself why do I feel
Like nobody truly understands
This magical bird just flew right beside me
As if he wished he could just hold my weary hand

In a moment of weakness I thought I should
Just keep going on my journey to figure things out
The special bird flew to the top of a new tree
As if he knew what it felt like to just wanna shout

Frustrated and confused as if nothing
In my life ever made sense
With my new friend flying beside me he taught me
Life is full of chances that knock us off our fence

Desperate to find a solution to my dreams and a place
Where my heart could finally call home
I stopped and looked at my unique friend
Who now loved me too much to ever let me go

Smiling and feeling assured that I had found
The missing link in my destined search for joy
My generous friend was a gift from God
More precious than any toy

At times when I know I need to regain my balance
When the world tries to confuse my mind
I just watch the red-winged black bird fly
From tree to tree with loving eyes and a heart so kind

In times of pain and times when I am not sure
If I can survive another crazy day
I can retreat to my safe haven and know there is
A true friend there who will never go away

Chapter 41 - The Soulmate Adventure

Magical Message #41: Sometimes the right adventure with the best company is what we need to embrace a fresh start.

Many times in life we often seek for an adventure because it is good to get away from the day to day routine. Sometimes we need a creative escape away from all our distresses because we all have times we need to rest and regroup. Every trip or journey we take in this life I feel fulfills a purpose, and I have found the most uplifting journeys are those connected to the spirit world.

When I think of the spirit world, I immediately think of the word soulmate as it reflects the powerful connection that exists between two hearts destined to love one another forever. As hard as it can be to be in the presence of someone we don't fully trust, I feel that sharing in the

company of a true soulmate is one of the most precious
blessings we can ever receive in this life.

The following poem, "The Soulmate Adventure", is all
about s spiritual journey shared by two like-minded souls
eager to escape their present existence into a world where
they feel they can truly be themselves and love one
another without judgment. Their lives before this
adventure have not always been the most rewarding, and
they realize that they must find a way to be together to fill
the void of despair that has haunted their lives for so
long. This poem is a poetic reflection of escape but more
importantly about love.

The Soulmate Adventure

I went on the kind of trip
That I wanted to last forever
I thought maybe if I close my eyes long enough
You and I would find the most precious treasure

So I waved a magic wand and
Asked you to make a great wish
You said just take me away from all
The chaos and help me find a life better than this

It was not too long you and I landed
On the most precious beach I had ever seen

MAGICAL LOVE MESSAGES BETWEEN KINDRED SPIRITS

We walked side by side through the fresh
Ocean waves meant to heal the past for you and me

You asked me to wave my magic wand
And grant you another wish to come true
The next thing I knew you and I were
Flying on a plane to a lovely place in Europe so totally cool

I felt you were having the time of your life
And ready for me to wave my magical wand again
The next thing I knew we were skydiving off a mountain
Into a water of hope that had no end

After this adventure I sensed you needed me
To wave my magic wand with great devotion
Then there we were having a picnic in a field of flowers
Loving each other with such emotion

I looked you in the eyes and you said
This adventure is too great to ever stop
I waved my magic wand taking us to Heaven
Where the angels cherished our souls quite a lot

It was this adventure where we walked the
Streets of gold hand in hand without a disruption
In the Heavenly world of faith, hope, and love
We discovered there was never an interruption

As I waved my magic wand again you and
I knew we had to go back to the real world

When we fell from Heaven we landed in a sea
Of the most harmonious melodies ever heard

While drifting aimlessly on a lake whose water
Kept our spirits able to survive
Together we could face the currents of life despite
Any misfortune trying to harm our way of life

When I lifted my magic wand to help us sleep
With the comforts of the most peaceful dream
Despite what came in this life I would always
Feel your heart embracing mine so blissfully

Chapter 42 - The Soulmate Protector

Magical Message #42: Sometimes the greatest joy we can feel is knowing that no matter where we are or what we are doing there is a spiritual force keeping us safe from harm.

Feeling safe is something that is important for all of us. We all want to know we have a safe place to fall when it seems the entire world is pulling us in many different directions. With all the demands we encounter in this life, I can't stress enough the importance of trying to find a place where you feel at peace.

The following poem, "The Soulmate Protector", is a poetic reflection of one soul's desire to escape her life, and even though she is unable to make this escape completely happen, she realizes she needs to feel the presence of someone who truly loves her.

Through deep thought and reflection, this person begins
to remember another time and place where she once lived
and discovered the most precious love she had ever
experienced. Through her memories and feelings of a
love that never left her side, the person in this story learns
she will never truly be alone.

The Soulmate Protector

I was feeling pulled in a million directions
Not knowing which way to turn
Sometimes I wondered when I could escape it all
And find someone who was truly concerned

There were times I just wanted to pull
The cover over my eyes and never wake up
Yet somehow I knew no matter how much I wanted to quit
I had to somehow believe in good luck

There were so many days I searched the world over
To find a love that would last forever
Somehow I knew someone was out there my soul
Was leading me to that wanted to be together

I fell back in time and was flooded with memories
Of an image of a spirit that never left my side
I could feel you whisper words of courage
That you'd love me through every lifetime

I tried to understand why I could not remember

MAGICAL LOVE MESSAGES BETWEEN KINDRED SPIRITS

The times I shared with the spirit I loved so much
Yet everyday I could feel the energy of a deeper love
Embracing my soul with the sweetest touch

Just when I thought all my hope
In life was completely over and gone
I could watch you walk into the room
With your caring eyes bringing me closer with a love song

During moments of weakness and times
When I felt like I could not make it through
I could feel you sending me energy to stay strong
When I often did not know what to do

When it seemed so many others had
A hidden agenda to try and break me down
I could just look right into your eyes and feel
Your warm, comforting presence all around

So many times I felt my life was going in
So many circles I just wanted to scream
Yet I could share energy with your loving heart
And know spiritually we made the best team

In moments when I felt like others
Were trying to keep us apart
I could just feel the strength of your love
Keeping me going when the whole world broke my heart

All the days I could smile with every bit of of joy

HEATHER D. WRIGHT

Within me I knew you could feel as well
It was as if the spiritual link between us
Enlightened our days with magical stories to tell

I feel that we share the kind of
Special love destiny that so many never find
You remain my true love that makes me feel
Truly cared for and loved all the time

I love you so much and appreciate all the things
You do just to make me feel truly safe
You are my soulmate protector that
I will cherish always in the most precious ways

Chapter 43 - The Soulmate Rescue

Magical Message #43: In times when we feel all alone are the times when God sends a spiritual gift through a special kind of rescue.

If there is one gift I feel we can both give and receive, it would be the gift of rescue. I feel we all want to be rescued from the pain and obstacles that try to hold us back. In many ways we all just want to feel protected knowing that no matter what happens someone or something will be there to catch us when we fall.

The following poem, "The Soulmate Rescue", is all about the special ways in which a lost soul finds help from the one person destined to love him forever which of course is his soulmate. Despite all the problems he has encountered, he finds solace knowing that God has sent a special soul his way to love and protect him.

I feel there is no better feeling than to meet the soul who
holds your heart and spirit close to his or her own
knowing there is someone in your corner to help you find
true peace through the best and worst of times.

The Soulmate Rescue

I could feel my world was
Unbalanced and tossing to and fro
Somewhere I could feel God asking me
To rescue you from the chaos and not let you go

Life had become more of a mystery
With others pulling you and me apart
Yet I knew that no matter what anyone did
I would love you forever with all my heart

I knew in this life obstacles were
Determined to keep us both confused
But deep in my soul I knew that I
Was destined to keep being true to you

There were moments in everyday
I felt lost not knowing which way to turn
Despite some of the misunderstandings between us
I knew we both had lessons to learn

Voices in my head were telling me that
At some point life would not be so bad

MAGICAL LOVE MESSAGES BETWEEN KINDRED SPIRITS

No matter how much the world let us down
I can feel your heart is still so sad

In my quest for the meaning of what love
Really is you always come to mind
In some ways I knew if my life were over today
I would still love you until the end of time

I thought about all the creative ways
In which God has brought us together
Now I know despite how broken our lives have been
Our love will endure the stormy weather

The dark energies of this world are on a mission
To keep us far from staying close
What they don't know is you and I possess
Unconditional love that is the secret only we know

The enemies to our connection want to make it look
At times like one of us hurt the other
Yet the spiritual ties that bind us keep me
Believing you will always be my spiritual lover

As the days pass and I reflect on
Everything you and I have had to face
God always shows me that even with the bad days
The good will come and we will be ok

In the depths of my heart and soul I know
You and I have a connection that will last forever

The magical ways in which we have learned to share
Our eternal love is our greatest treasure

Chapter 44 - The Special Friend that Took a Lost Child By the Hand

---

Magical Message #44: We must make every moment count in this life as we never know when it will be our last.

I have never understood how someone could take the life of another without feeling some level of remorse. After watching so many news stories about a gunman opening fire on an innocent classroom of students and teachers, I felt maybe I should do something to express my own level of concern.

The following poem, "The Special Friend that Took a Lost Child by the Hand", is my own way of putting myself in the place of an innocent child who goes to school enjoying her time with her teachers and friends. However, in an instant her whole life changes as a strange man walks into this little girl's classroom opening fire only to kill so many innocent children along with their teacher.

As with any tragedy in life, this poem shows that there is life after death and a way for this innocent child who I am portraying to see her fellow classmates and teachers whose lives were also cut short. It is a bittersweet tale of love and loss as the souls whose lives were taken too soon find peace on the other side, even though all they can do is surround their family and friends who are left behind with a spirit of great love. If anything, this poetic story is not only about surviving loss, but learning to find comfort with other like-minded survivors.

The Special Friend that Took a Lost Child by the Hand

I was just a child getting
Ready to go to school
My mother and father gave me a hug and a kiss
And said I know your teachers will be good to you

With a smile on my face I could not wait
To see what I would learn in class
I was just seven years old but I had a desire
To explore the world with a joy I hoped would last

It was a nice little school where I had
So many friends I had made along the way

MAGICAL LOVE MESSAGES BETWEEN KINDRED SPIRITS

Some of them stood by my side and
Made me happy every passing day

Yet there was something about this one day
In December that seemed to make me scared
All of a sudden my sunny world seemed to turn dark
And overcome with sudden despair

I looked around and saw a dark figure
Come charging into my class with gunshots firing around
I was so scared that I prayed and asked God to protect
My teacher, my friends, and me so we would not be
gunned down

Before I could finish my prayer
I felt the deepest wound pierce my fragile heart
What was once a normal way of life for me
Ended tragically leaving me cold and in the dark

I lay helpless in a meadow of colorful flowers
In the most beautiful world I had ever seen
As soon as I looked up, I saw a beautiful hand
Of hope reaching down to comfort me

When I took this miraculous hand
Of a stranger I did not know
I asked him when I could see
My mom and dad and get to go home

This special friend said I am here now to give

HEATHER D. WRIGHT

You comfort and take you to a brand new place
In this new world you can learn all the spiritual truths
Of life and always feel truly safe

I was crying because I already missed
My family and friends that I had just seen
My new special friend said please do not cry
Because there is no reason to be afraid or feel misery

As I walked through the meadow hand in hand
With a special friend unlike any I had known
He waved a magic wand to let me see
A new world that would become my new, safe home

I asked my special friend if I could
Go back to the life I knew best
My special friend just wiped my tears away and said
Your life has ended but your soul is now at rest

I could not understand why I had to leave
And not get to enjoy longer years of my life
My special friend said you will be a little angel
To those needing comfort in the midst of their strife

I asked my new special friend what
His name was because I was very scared
He looked at me with the most spiritual eyes of love
Saying I am your Heavenly Father who will always care

As we kept walking I wanted to know if

MAGICAL LOVE MESSAGES BETWEEN KINDRED SPIRITS

Being an angel would be hard to do
My Heavenly Father said just keep saying your prayers
And you will seek those who need love and kindness too

When we reached another part
Of this spiritual place where I felt at peace
I was greeted by other friends of mine and my teacher
I loved with new hope and much relief

They greeted me with such love and happiness
Much like what I knew when I was in class
Somehow this new world was different and now
We have a God making sure our pain did not last

As sad as we were to leave behind
Our parents who loved us so
Our Heavenly Father gave us the ability to breathe words
Of comfort so our parents would feel their children grow

Chapter 45 - The Special Friendship Between a Seagull and a Starfish

---

Magical Message #45: Knowing you have a true friend you can trust beyond measure is one of the most precious gifts you could ever receive.

In this life it is easy to get discouraged and to question why. Sometimes it can seem that nobody truly knows or understands us. Then one day we encounter someone or something that shows us what true friendship really means.

The following poem, "The Special Friendship Between a Seagull and a Starfish", is a special story about two creatures of the sea befriending one another and becoming the best of friends. Each of these creatures have both endured many trials in their lives so to find

each other turns out to be a special blessing for both of
them.

In the same fashion, that moment you discover the one
like-minded soul who understands you on a deep level is
truly one of the most special blessings you could ever
receive in this life. In a world where it is hard to find
someone you can trust, there is nothing more beautiful
than finding the one friend who accepts you for who you
are and believes in you.

The Special Friendship Between a Seagull and a Starfish

Once upon a time on a magical coastal shore
In a distant land far and away
There were two special creatures God breathed
Life into that came to love each other in a creative way

One of nature's finest was a seagull that
Had been flying high and low searching for a friend
Somehow he needed someone to cherish and
Protect until his life came to an end

On a warm, sunny day on a beach where
A cool breeze embraced the waves crashing on the beach
The admirable seagull noticed a brown little starfish
On the shore who was within his loving reach

As the seagull flew close to the shore to watch
The starfish struggle to make it back to the sea

The seagull walked right up to her and said
I am here for you and promise to never leave

The weary starfish cried out you do not know
How tired I am of trying so hard
The seagull said at times I wish I could fly away
So nothing could ever damage my often sad heart

Amazed that the seagull seemed to understand
The sadness this starfish seemed to feel
The starfish just looked at him with tears in her eyes
Saying she always wanted a friend that was real

The seagull knew the starfish wanted to get back
To the water where it could swim to its heart's delight
When the starfish cried please help me the seagull knew
How it felt to be in constant flight

Little by little the seagull pushed his friend with his beak
Closer to the waves the starfish called home
Even though the starfish was too weak try on his own
The seagull said I promise to never let you go

After pushing the seagull to keep fighting
To live and to never give up
The starfish made it back to the water feeling
She would now have some much better luck

As the starfish kept swimming around in the
Ocean water feeling more joyful and at peace

MAGICAL LOVE MESSAGES BETWEEN KINDRED SPIRITS

She noticed her friend the seagull flew right above
Looking out for her putting her spirit at ease

When the sun would set and the night would
Once again make her visit to the sandy coast
The seagull stood on the shore reassuring his friend
He would always love her and protect her the most

Chapter 46 – The Time Machine Back to a Fairy Tale Kind of Life

---

Magical Message #46: It is ok to wish for the ability to revisit another time and place where we feel most accepted and loved.

Ever since I was a child, there have been two things that I have always loved...fairy tales and time machines. I always thought that it would be good to just live a fairy tale kind of life and having a time machine take you back to a special place in your own past or somewhere different is equally fascinating.

The following poem, "The Time Machine Back to a Fairy Tale Kind of Life", is all about one person's journey back to a previous life where he once lived with two people he loved dearly...his trusted soulmate and his special cat. Through this poetic journey of love and friendship a beautiful story is told of one soul's travel back into the

arms and presence of those with whom is heart and soul
has never forgotten.

As I have learned, it's ok to escape into a world of
imagination sometimes because that is when we discover
what makes us most happy.

The Time Machine Back to A Fairy Tale Kind of Life

I finally closed my eyes
And made an admirable wish
Somehow I knew there was a life I lived
Much greater than this

As I took a deep breath I asked
God to send me a time machine
When I opened my eyes there one stood
So charming and so meant for me

When I jumped inside to take control
Of this most fascinating wheel
I felt a spiritual energy pulling me back to a time
When love was real

Before I knew it the time machine took me
To a place full of sunshine and fields of flowers
The moment I stepped onto the ground I knew
It was blessed with some magical powers

I walked through the flowery fields

As the sun cast bright rays of light so true
Then to my pleasant surprise I caught
A most precious glimpse of you

There you and I sat having a picnic with our
Good friend the cat who was our treasure
Sharing a lunch with our animal friend
Was our most cherished pleasure

In the afternoon I watched us both walk
The fields of great dreams with our cat by our side
You and I talked for hours after helping bring food
And water to those struggling to survive

As I continued to observe every minute
Of our most joyous interaction
The cat we loved so much seemed happy
We could help each other with the most positive reactions

We were close friends sharing a special kind of love
Even our families did not understand
As I watched everyday pass I could feel love
Kept us strong when we were on sinking sand

In the bright of day when we were free to run
And play and share from our hearts without end
We never left each others' side and always
Had our special cat comforting us like a good friend.

During the dark of night when we both

MAGICAL LOVE MESSAGES BETWEEN KINDRED SPIRITS

Were in our homes fast asleep
I could feel a spiritual closeness keep us strongly
Connected as our dreams united us in peace

I noticed that in this lifetime nobody
Was able to keep us apart
We remained forever united with the strongest kind
Of love that kept us warm at heart

As I watched the scenes of this life with
You, me, and our faithful cat always there
I decided to take this affectionate energy back to
My present life when I needed someone to care

I got back into my time machine even though
I really did not want to leave
Though I could not recreate this time I knew
I wanted to return and stay close to you so faithfully

When my time machine took me home I was greeted
By a kitten much like the one you and I loved
Then I realized I was meant to cherish and protect you
Forever with spiritual ties from God above

Chapter 47 - The True Soul Friend

———————

Magical Message #47: Sometimes the most unlikely friendships are the ones that warm our hearts the most.

I feel animals are truly sent by God to bring peace into our lives. Even though I love the comfort of a good domestic cat or dog, I have often found the random animals in nature can surprise us when in need of some loving affection. As someone who loves to be outside, I often find myself drawn to the creatures of the wild, as I feel they bring messages of hope and healing.

The following poem, "The True Soul Friend", is a story of a person lost in the wilderness of despair looking for a friend to help him find his way back home. In the midst of his agony, a lovely fawn comes right to his side, offering him a chance to see the beauty life can bring even when it seems so hard to believe and endure.

———

As the poem indicates, never take for granted the things
that cross your path unexpectedly as they can truly help
you heal when you need it most.

The True Soul Friend

In the middle of a dark and frightening night
I found myself lost and far from home
All the vultures of the wilderness wanted to keep
My spirit feeling lifeless and cold

I felt the whole world was spinning and
I wondered when I would break free
So I prayed and asked God to send me a sign
Of hope things would get better for me

In the wilderness of broken dreams and false hopes
A baby fawn soon came by my side
There was something about the way it came to me
Out of nowhere that just made me smile

I felt as if everything in my life had been a road
Of constant setbacks I could not comprehend
Yet somehow this little fawn came right to me
When I needed to feel the love of true soul friend

I looked him in the eyes and asked him why
My life always seemed to be such a constant battle
His caring eyes said don't lose hope as true lessons
Are learned when life comes unraveled

I gently stroked his gentle, white spotted coat
Because I needed to feel his comforting touch
Even though I had so many unlucky breaks in life
I could feel he loved me so much

I watched him walk around me in just
Complete awe of his beauty and grace
Despite my own inner frustrations I was
So impressed by his truly peaceful ways

I wanted to stay right where I was in my life
Because I was so afraid of change
Yet this sweet fawn said come follow me and trust
Greater joys await the rest of your days

I thought about staying right where I was
Just because I was fearful of making a rash move
But as the precious fawn headed out of the grim forest
Into the light I felt his words were true

After so many months of walking around
In darkness I could finally see the light
The fawn of the forest was God's message to
Keep the faith to know everything would be all right

As I followed my true soul friend I was too weak
To keep up with his steady, strong pace
Yet he just walked right by my side throughout my journey
Protecting me with his love and kind ways

Chapter 48 - To Mom and Dad With Love

_____

Magical Message #48: Being blessed with the unconditional love of two parents is one of the most precious gifts God could ever give us.

I have to say that I have been blessed with the best parents you could ever ask for. From the time I was a child until my adult years, both my mom and dad have always been there for me. There have been times I felt I had nobody to turn to, and despite my own problems, they have loved and supported me through every circumstance I have faced.

At this juncture in my life, my parents are still the ones I love and admire with great respect, and yet they have become dear friends to me as well. I can rely on them as any child would, and yet, I can talk with both of them as I would with any good friend who has your back no matter what.

The following poem, "To Mom and Dad With Love", depicts the loving bond I have developed with my parents over the years and that I still cherish to this day. In many ways, I feel it reflects the great love that should always exist between parents and their children. As I have learned, life is short, and we should always honor our parents for the life they gave us as well the strong foundation of support they want us to experience.

To Mom and Dad With Love

I just wanted to say I love you
For always being there for me
No matter how good or bad my days are
You have always loved me so faithfully

I just wanted to say I love you for always
Encouraging me to do my best
Even when I feel like giving up you just give me
Strength to enjoy life with much needed rest

I just wanted to say I love you for always
Helping me find a way to be strong
There are times I think I cannot get through a day
But your love for me never goes wrong

I just wanted to say I love you for giving

MAGICAL LOVE MESSAGES BETWEEN KINDRED SPIRITS

My heart hope to keep my dreams alive
When times are tough you just keep inspiring me
To keep trying hard all the time

I just wanted to say I love you for seeing
The very spark of joy in my soul
Even when I feel sad you are always there for me
And never will let me go

I just wanted to say I love you for helping me
Learn that having faith will always see me through
You just know the right words to say
To keep my heart feeling strong and true

I just wanted to say I love you for taking the time
To really listen to me when I am in need
You give great advice to help me walk the right path
And keep practicing good deeds

I just wanted to say I love you for helping me
To make good choices when I feel confused
Even when others try to throw me off track
You tell me to relax and keep my cool

I just wanted to say I love you for taking
The time to always tell you me you care
No matter how many times others let me down
I know you will always be there

I just wanted to say I love you for telling me

HEATHER D. WRIGHT

The truth when others tell me just what I want to hear
Even when everyone around me gives me bad advice
Your wise words are always clear

I just wanted to say I love you for giving me
Courage to face my hardships without worry
You help me to keep my smile and to stay calm
When the rest of the world is in a hurry

I just wanted to say I love you for sharing with me
All the lessons you have learned
Now I know that despite what happens you will
Let me share my own stories with great concern

I just wanted to say I love you for teaching me
The true art of showing respect and admiration
When the rest of the world is negative your positive
Focus keeps me feeling free from desolation

I just wanted to say I love you
For always standing by my side
You are more than my mother and father but dear friends
That are my protectors and forever guides

I just wanted to say I love you
From the very depths of my heart
Throughout all the changing seasons
I love the bond connecting us despite where we are

Chapter 49 - Two Trees Linked by a Loving Connection

Magical Message #49: There are some bonds and connections so strong that no destructive force of nature could ever break.

I have often found it quite amazing how we can feel drawn to different people for various reasons. When I was much younger, I would often dismiss why I felt drawn to some people more than others as I did not understand it. I thought maybe it was because in that particular moment I had something in common with the person to whom I felt drawn. As I grew older, I have found myself drawn to certain people for reasons that I may not have always understood, but I realized in one way or another there was a reason I felt such a powerful bond so I learned to trust it.

The following poem "Two Trees Linked by a Loving

Connection", is a story about two trees who seem to have strong roots, yet they both find themselves depending on each other for love and support. In this story of love and friendship, the two trees realize they feel drawn to each other, not because they are in close proximity to one another, but because their hearts and souls connect in the most spiritual and beautiful of ways.

As life unfolds, I have learned not to take for granted spiritual bonds because these emotional ties are truly the most precious and rewarding gifts we could ever receive knowing that there is a connection upon which we can count through the best and worst of times.

Two Trees Linked by a Loving Connection

One upon a time there were
Two special trees so completely linked
It seemed they stood rooted in a great love
For each other and always remained in sync

One tree stood strong and whispered to her friend
Standing right by her side
She cried you are just what I need
When I feel lost and lonely inside

As the other tree's branches swayed
With such grace and ease

MAGICAL LOVE MESSAGES BETWEEN KINDRED SPIRITS

He let the delicate touch of his leaves embrace
His friend's branches with the most gentle peace

There were days the rains would come
To refresh the trees where they stood
During stormy weather the trees had faith
Their mutual trust would keep them feeling very good

After a long hard night of rough wind and thunder
That seemed would never stop
Both trees looked at each other knowing together
They could survive quite a lot

In the most sunny of days when birds of all kinds
Came to perch on the limbs of either tree
The two trees just smiled at one another
As nature's finest was drawn to their loving fantasy

Many times people walked past these trees
And felt drawn to their calming energies
It seemed as if those passing by felt the love they shared
Even calm their own inner miseries

Some people stood right in front of these trees
As a breeze blew their branches to and fro
In the middle of life's tough moments you could feel
They loved each other too much to ever let go

After sunny days and even times when
The mild storms of spring and summer would pass

Fierce winds came in the fall as the trees lost
Their colorful leaves that one day they would get back

When both trees lost their leaves in the winter
That colored their magical world so much
Each let the warmth of his branches touch the other
With the most graceful and heartfelt love

As the cold snow and sleet often came resting
On the delicate limbs of both trees each morning
Each one just remained beautiful and bold
As if they could beat any odds no matter the warning

When the cold winter days and nights
Faded once again into the tapestry of spring
The leaves budded once again on each tree
As if they were linked together by a loving destiny

The gentle warmth of spring days once again
Spread its light on the trees that were so close
Through all the seasons of life their caring branches
Embraced the other with forever love and hope

Chapter 50 - With Love From Mr. Goodbar

Magical Message #50: Sometimes something that tastes so sweet can feel so good and help you feel truly loved and understood.

Ever since I was a child, I have always had a sweet tooth. I often found myself lost in a candy store feeling drawn to all the different candy in my midst. The one candy bar I always liked best was Mr. Goodbar. After all, with a name like that one, how could you not want to try a bite?

One day, as I was in a creative state of mind, and of course after I had eaten a Mr. Goodbar, I thought about the concept of love. Then I thought how awesome would it be to receive love from a special Mr. Goodbar knowing it is the kind of love you have always treasured and wanted most.

The following poem, "With Love from Mr. Goodbar", is a simple but loving story about how just one bite of a candy bar could help someone in need of comfort and love in that particular moment appreciate the simpler pleasures of life.

After all, love is the one gift that truly makes this life worth living.

With Love from Mr. Goodbar

I was craving something sweet
That I so needed to keep me strong
I felt defeated because I just wanted
To make right all I had ever done wrong

I went to the store thinking there was
A candy bar there just for me
The next thing I knew the lure of Mr. Goodbar
Excited my spirit so positively

When I unwrapped the yellow candy bar
I took a bite of one little square
As the chocolate melted in my mouth
Mr. Goodbar made me feel someone did really care

I took another bite and could feel
The chocolate appeal to my senses
Mr. Goodbar wanted me to know
I would regain control of all my struggling defenses

MAGICAL LOVE MESSAGES BETWEEN KINDRED SPIRITS

The next bite I took was so precious
It made me feel life was really sweet
Mr. Goodbar cried out I will protect your soul
When the world makes you feel weak

So I was curious to know more and took
Another bite that just melted in my mouth
Mr. Goodbar whispered don't worry
So much and trust it will all work out

My hungry spirit took another bite
Hoping to feel the taste of something good
Mr. Goodbar said stick with me and
I will make sure life works out as it should

Feeling eager to take another bite
To find the next treat I was meant to receive
Mr. Goodbar kindly shared I should savor
Each moment and let life be good to me

As I took the next bite I was wondering
If I would ever fully satisfy my desire to survive
Mr. Goodbar said come find me again
When all you wanna do is sit down and cry

I reached the last few bites and felt
I did not want the great taste to end
Mr. Goodbar said I know you feel alone
But in me you will always have a true friend

HEATHER D. WRIGHT

After I finished the candy bar I realized
Some desires we are meant to embrace
The love from Mr. Goodbar encouraged me
To appreciate what matters most everyday

Afterword

After your journey into the special world of love and friendship, I hope *Magical Love Messages Between Kindred Spirits* helped you believe that with love anything is truly possible. I feel love is the most beautiful force in the universe as without it we all feel we are just walking along the path of life feeling alone and lost. Through all the commentary and poems of this book, I hope your heart and soul feels without question the kind of love we all long for that is truly spiritual and unconditional.

Throughout my journey during my time in this world, I have always been in love with love all my life. Even with all the ups and downs it has brought me, I would not trade this special feeling for anything in the world and certainly appreciate an honest and loyal love that is beyond human measure.

As you go through all the days of your life, I hope you find yourself reminded of the warm sentiments *Magical Love*

AFTERWORD

Messages Between Kindred Spirits holds for both the old and young at heart. Remember the best gift you can ever give and receive is simply love, and when you can share that love and friendship with another like-minded spirit such as yourself, well let me just say, you have found an eternal golden treasure to make you happy for a lifetime.

About the Author

After writing my books, *Spiritual Whispers to the Soul* and *Living and Learning from the Healing Waters of Courage*, I decided that my current book, *Magical Love Messages Between Kindred Spirits*, would be my chance to share my heartfelt sentiments in the realm of love and friendship.

As we all know, life is hard enough so I felt I would let the words of this book stir the heart strings of those needing to feel a deeper kind of love and friendship that is truly felt between kindred souls whether through family, friends, a romantic partner, a pet, or even an acquaintance destined to become closer.

My goal is to continue to write more books under my publishing name, Colorful Spirit Publishing, in the hopes to keep encouraging the hearts and souls of many looking for some happiness in their lives.

For more information on where to find all my books,

ABOUT THE AUTHOR

please visit my website at www.colorfulspirit.com or feel free to email me at hwright@colorfulspirit.com. You will also find many of my individual writings for sale at my online store at www.colorfulspiritgifts.com. I hope that the words I continue to write inspire you to know everything has a way of working out for the best as along as true love is in the mix.

www.ingramcontent.com/pod-product-compliance
Lightning Source LLC
Chambersburg PA
CBHW031545040426
42452CB00006B/193